# THE PATTERN OF LIFE

ALFRED ADLER

# THE PATTERN OF LIFE

*Edited by W. Béran Wolfe, M. D.*

Preface II by Bernard H. Shulman, M.D.

Cosmopolitan Book Corporation
NEW YORK, MCMXXX

*Printed in the U. S. A. by J. J. Little & Ives Co.*
*New York*

Second Edition

Library of Congress Catalog Card
Number 81-71160
Printed in the United States of America
ISBN 0-918560-28-4

# *CONTENTS*

# THE PATTERN OF LIFE

# PREFACE II

*The Pattern of Life* was originally published by Cosmopolitan Book Corporation in 1930 with the introductory essay by the editor, W. Beran Wolfe that is included in the present edition. Beran Wolfe was a physician co-worker of Adler's who published several books on popular topics, all now out of print. These books were: *How To Be Happy Though Human, Nervous Breakdown: It's Cause and Cure, A Woman's Best Years* and *Successful Living.* As the catchy titles indicate, these were written primarily for the layman; however, the first two were good enough to be used in course work at the Alfred Adler Institute of Chicago until they became no longer available.

*The Pattern of Life* consists of transcripts of case readings and client interviews by Adler during his lecture series at the New School of Social Research in New York during the 1929 lecture series. It was one of Adler's first experiences with American clients and one wonders how much a possible language difficulty interfered with his counseling. Cases were brought to Adler by psychologists, physicians and school teachers and he used this material for combination lecture-demonstrations in this setting. The person who brought the case would present the history, which was not included in this book. Adler would then review the history and make diagnostic guesses whenever some point in the history seemed revealing to him. A discussion of the case would follow, then the case would be brought in for a short interview, Adler would give some advice and sometimes another discussion would follow. Most of the cases in the book are children; thus, the parents were also often seen. This format was followed by Dreikurs in his demonstrations in family education centers and has become a standard way of teaching family counseling among Adlerians.

The cases give Adler an opportunity to give an outline of childhood behavior problems and is perhaps the most valuable part of the book. The case readings also show how Adler used his technique of making guesses as he went through the case until he had constructed a plausible picture of the client's personality and an understanding of the behavior.

The acutal interviews may be disappointing to those who have watched other counselors interact with clients. Many of the children respond only with a "yes" or "no" to Adler's questions. There is no mention of the "recognition reflex" or other responses displayed by the child. There is no systematic determination of the immediate goal of the child's misbehavior. Nevertheless, Adler's interviews are useful in teaching us how he actually worked with cases. The bare transcript gives no hint of Adler's interviewing style. He was, from all reports, a friendly, non-threatening interviewer who put the clients at ease in front of the audience. The interviews with children are very short. In them, Adler is constantly optimistic and encouraging and one wonders what effect this really had on the children.

One senses Adler's friendliness in the interviews and wishes that he had let the clients talk a little more. The audience only observes and does not interact with the client, but sometimes asks Adler questions which he answers.

A word of caution: The language in the book is that of 1930. Thus, when Beran Wolfe and Adler talk about the "neurotic" they mean the same thing that Adler meant in his treatise *The Neurotic Constitution*—a person who has become discouraged by the interaction between life events and his own life style and who has developed "useless" (non-constructive) behaviors.

Beran Wolfe's preface is a mini-course in the fundamentals of Individual Psychology and should be read with that thought in mind.

BHS
1978

# *ADLER AND OUR NEUROTIC WORLD*

W. Beran Wolfe, M. D.

THE art of understanding human nature is the art of understanding the dynamic patterns of human conduct. Alfred Adler has given us the key to this understanding in his monumental contributions to modern psychology, but before the compilation of this volume of case histories the student of the methods of Individual Psychology has been compelled to search for his case material among the German publications of Adler and his pupils. Many of these published cases deal with conditions germane to continental environments, but puzzling to American readers. The principles and practice of Individual Psychology, however, are universally valid in their application, as this volume of purely American cases demonstrates. The essential unity of all human conduct is amply adduced by the success of the Viennese psychologist and educator in the analysis and treatment of these cases brought to his clinic, without previous selection or limitation, at the New School of Social Research, during his lecture season of 1929. They are typical of cases found in the schools and child-guidance clinics of every large American city. Some of the cases were brought in by New

York physicians, some by psychologists, but the majority by New York school teachers who were puzzled by problem children under their care.

All of the cases were worked up more or less thoroughly according to an outline for the study of problem children written originally for the child-guidance clinics which Dr. Adler established in Vienna. Although for the sake of brevity the headings have not been incorporated in the text, the arrangement will be obvious to any student who desires to prepare a case history for study. The method of presentation was as follows: a physician or teacher who had studied a problem child prepared the history according to the protocol. Dr. Adler, without having seen the child or previously discussing the case with the teacher, read the case history, sentence by sentence, making his deductions as the case progressed. Occasionally Dr. Adler was misled by a statement in the protocol, but in the vast majority of instances he built up a dynamic picture of the child's personality, often predicting the findings with uncanny insight into the ways of a child's soul, always illuminating the history with his gentle sympathy for the actors in the human drama under discussion.

After the record had been analyzed with the finesse of a psychiatric detective weighing clues, a brief discussion of the child's situation followed, and a summary of the aims of psychotherapy or guidance outlined. The parents of the child were then brought into the lecture room and questioned and instructed before the class. Finally the child himself was brought in, and the situation was discussed with him in simple, kindly language. The follow-up work, indicated by the analysis, was then entrusted to the teacher or physician who had presented the history. From time to time, during the course of lectures, reports of progress were brought in, and the reactions of the children discussed.

Not all the cases were finally successful in their readjustment, failures being due sometimes to the ignorance and lack of cooperation of parents whose neuroses remained unresolved despite the efforts of teachers and psychiatrists to change their attitudes toward their children. Other causes of slow progress were deplorable economic situations, intercurrent diseases, or difficulties which served to restore the original situation in which the neurosis occurred. Some of the cases showed temporary improvement but presented new sets of symptoms under new conditions, which required continued psychotherapy until the parents had gained a more complete insight into the dynamics of the child's behavior, or the child had exhausted his repertoire of neurotic tricks. One of our own cases which showed excellent progress under intensive treatment and reeducation, relapsed when the child was faced by the insuperable problem of an old-style school teacher, whose discouragement and deprecation in a few days destroyed the results of months of painstaking work. Yet the great majority of these cases showed definite improvement, and a considerable number a complete change of pattern.

Readers of this book should realize that it is not a comprehensive treatise on psychotherapy, but rather an outline of childhood neuroses and a key to the art of reading case histories. Its chief value lies in acquainting all those who have to deal with children and adults with the dynamic patterns of human conduct. The technique of cure can no more be taught by such a volume than the art of etching can be taught by a treatise on the various physical and chemical processes that comprise the technique of preparing and printing a copper-plate. The book will have fulfilled its purpose if it succeeds in encouraging all who study its pages to view human beings not as static machines designated by labels, but as moving, living, purpose-fulfilling entities striving for significance and security in a perplexing world.

### SOME BASIC ASSUMPTIONS IN INDIVIDUAL PSYCHOLOGY

The principles and practice of Individual Psychology have been treated exhaustively in works devoted to the scientific discussion of Dr. Alfred Adler's contributions to modern psychology. At the risk of fatiguing readers who have already mastered the theories of Individual Psychology, it seems especially advisable to include a short and necessarily incomplete outline of these principles for readers to whom "The Pattern of Life" is a first introduction to Adler's work, lest the cases in the book seem unrelated and incomprehensible.

The concept of the unity of the human personality, which is the foundation of Individual Psychology, is neither new nor unique to Alfred Adler's psychology. The Greek dramatists considered this unity essential long before the birth of Christ. The unknown writer of the nursery rhyme of Humpty Dumpty stated the case for this indestructible unity of living organisms when he proclaimed that all the king's horses and all the king's men could not reassemble a broken egg. Were it not for this unity, no psychologist could predict human behavior as Adler has been able to predict the conduct of a child after reading a case protocol. It is philosophically impossible to conceive of more than one soul in a body, just as it is impossible to believe that human conduct is solely the *result* of certain motivating and activating drives and instincts, since no one can predict the relative potency of such drives and instincts. If each human being were no more than the haphazard resultant of the blind interaction of imponderable energies, a systematic psychology would be as impossible as a science of chemistry in which the chemical elements changed their valence from day to day. Great poets, shrewd old women, novelists, successful generals, and business men know that this unity of the human organism is the *sine qua non* of human understanding.

The second great principle of Adler's psychology is that the unit organism is a dynamic whole, moving through a definite life pattern toward a definite goal. "The goal of life is the maintenance of life," as Rémy de Gourmont wrote in his "Physique de l'Amour." It is this goal which differentiates living matter from dead matter. A sand pile has no goal. If you remove a few shovelfuls of sand from a sand pile, its essential nature is not changed. It remains a sand pile. But a living organism, be it a one-celled amœba, a humming-bird, or giraffe, has a goal of life, and its entire organization and way of life is appropriate to the attainment of that goal. You cannot remove an essential portion of a living organism without changing it into an amorphous congeries of inert cells.

Each living organism has a definite life pattern and a definite and characteristic technique of combating the environment in order to maintain its life and goal. The complexity of the pattern varies with the organism's capability of change and adaptation, and for this reason the patterns of human behavior are much more complicated than the patterns of an oak tree, a comparatively immobile and fixed organism. What we call soul, or psyche, in a purely biological sense, is the function of adaptation, of apperception, of the mobilization of resources, and the maintenance of life by an offensive-defensive strategy of living.

What is the goal of human life? We shall not attempt an essay in the metaphysics of human existence here. Viewed objectively and dispassionately we see that every human organism strives for a measure of security and totality which makes continued existence tolerable. The goal of the human race is the maintenance of the human race.

Just as every living species has its characteristic technique of self-preservation—the tortoise its shell, the chameleon its adaptability, the hare its fleetness, the tiger its ferocity and strength—so the human race has its characteristic method of self-preservation. This technique we call communal life, society, civilization. Millennia of living have proved this the best method. So far as archeological researches can determine, human beings have always lived in groups. The recent discoveries of the most primitive man, the Pekin man, showed that ten millions of years ago our ancestors were already living in a community.

Because it is no more possible to conceive of an isolated man than it is possible to conceive of a short-necked giraffe, it is obvious that every psychology, every science of human behavior, must be a social psychology. The fate of the individual is inextricably linked with the fate of his group. This is a fundamental principle of Adler's Individual Psychology. To understand a human being you must understand his relative situation in the human group in which he moves. He cannot be isolated in a laboratory and watched and observed as the behaviorists have attempted to do, because in the moment he is isolated he no longer acts as a human being, but as a caged animal. He is no longer, strictly speaking, a human being. All human behavior, therefore, must be taken in its social relativity if it is to be understood. Just as a pine tree develops differently at the snow line from the way it does in a sunny valley, so the human being will act differently if his social environment is changed.

The social life of the human race is an outgrowth of its weakness. Communal existence was probably the quickest and most effective way our ancestors could find to protect themselves. The pattern of the human race has been a pattern beginning in individual weakness, moving toward a goal of comparative security in social solidarity. All the strengths of the human race fit into this pattern; all its weaknesses are derived from the danger of isolation. Just as in our structural growth we recapitulate the evolution of all living matter, from a single cell to an organized unity of interdependent tissues and organs, so the psychological growth of the individual is a recapitulation of the psychological organization of the race.

Every human being begins life as a relatively helpless, impotent, dependent parasite. Without the aid of his parents, the first community of the family, the human infant would perish miserably in a few hours. Under the fostering influence of parents the individual child grows in power and ability. During his growth he is a virtual parasite of the society that nurtures him.

With maturity the normal individual has developed adequate powers to begin life as a contributing member of his social group. In affirming the multiplex bonds that bind human being to human being, the normal mature individual gains a measure of peace, security, and a sense of totality and validity which make life worth living. The more of these bridges that a human being builds to his fellows the more secure he is. Speech, common sense, reason, logic, ideas, sympathy, love, science, art, religion, politics, responsibility, self-reliance, honesty, usefulness, play, love of nature, and the like, are among the most important bridges. To forego any of these techniques of communal life is to be only partially successful as a human being, to be only partially secure.

Unfortunately for us this normal pattern of development does not always occur. The reasons for its failure derive from an important biological characteristic of the human infant. The young of other species also go through a period of helplessness and dependence upon their parents, but as their physical powers grow, a parallel development of their mental capabilities occurs. A kitten that is capable of recognizing a mouse, can stalk it, catch it, and eat it. But in the human infant there is a gross disproportion between the perceptual faculties and the motor capabilities. The baby can recognize the fact that it is dependent upon its mother for food and warmth and protection. It knows that the mother is capable of many necessary activities which lie beyond its powers. A father appears as a huge and relatively omnipotent giant. The world about the baby moves according to ineluctable laws. Darkness and light, food and hunger, speech, locomotion, are vassals of the strange adults who move so surely and knowingly through the baby's cosmos. But the young child realizes his relative weakness. The human baby is the only living animal that experiences his own inadequacy because his mind develops faster than his body. It is in this situation that the feeling of inferiority, a cornerstone of Individual Psychology, is created.

Far from being a handicap, the inferiority feeling has proved itself the most cogent stimulus for the development of the human race. The telescope and the microscope would never have been invented if our human eyes were as powerful as the eagle's; the phonograph, the radio, the telephone, could never have existed without a need for better communication between human beings; the art of the perfumer and the virtuosity of the chef are our compensations for the blunting of primitive sensory perceptions far better developed in the "lower" animals. The very structure of our civilization, from newspapers to skyscrapers, from airplanes to symphony orchestras, from steam shovels to silk stockings, is the resultant of this primitive need for the compensation of human frailties.

The inferiority feeling to which every human being is heir because of his physical and biological constellation in the cosmos need not therefore be an individual liability. Man's history is replete with records of his conquest of inferiority. Genius is probably no more than the expression of the urge to compensate for an individual defect in terms of social contribution. Every work of genius bears this mark of social usefulness. When we speak of genius we are inclined to forget those unsung men who invented the lever, the wheel, the ax, the musical reed, weaving, writing, and the like, and remember solely our modern geniuses who have but combined these elements in some novel form. The true history of human genius is the history of the caveman's struggle for existence.

Each human being is capable of elaborating his personal defects into a useful contribution to society, yet a superficial survey of our society indicates that only a small proportion of the human race has gained the courage to effect such compensations. Our neurotics far outnumber our geniuses. How can we account for the failure of useful compensation?

Unfortunately for the human race, a variety of factors militate against the optimum compensation of the inferiority feeling in social adjustment and in useful work. The first of these factors that intensify the inferiority feeling until it crystallizes in an inferiority complex is the factor of physical defect. If in addition to his normal weakness the human infant experiences a special weakness in the form of a defective apparatus, his struggle for significance is made more difficult. This inferiority may be an actual inferiority of certain organs or organ systems of his body. It may, however, be an unimportant physical anomaly, medically unimportant, but socially embarrassing, such as abnormal fatness, thinness, albinism, moles, red hair, bow legs, facial hair, and the like. Ugliness is a special case in point, and, strange as it may seem, exceptional beauty may eventually lead to an inferiority complex because the beautiful child believes that his beauty is the only contribution which society requires of him.

The second group of factors that intensify the inferiority feeling deal with the social, religious, and economic condition of the individual. Members of any minority group, whether social, religious, or economic, suffer an accentuation of their inferiority feeling because of the additional difficulties of the world, contact with sordidness, vice, and crime. Great riches, however, may also have a disastrous effect, because the proper stimulus to work is so frequently lacking where a child grows up in an atmosphere of affluence.

A third set of factors that may intensify the inferiority feeling of the child derive from his family constellation. This group is important, because no child escapes its influence. The only child derives his inferiority complex from his abnormal importance in the family, and his poor training for social adjustment. His life is all too frequently a search for the lost paradise of his youth. The oldest child, having been an only child, and displaced by a younger rival, may be so discouraged by his fall from power that he can never muster sufficient courage to attack the problems of existence objectively. The second child, although he grows up in the same house, imbibes the same milk, sleeps in the same room as the older child, nevertheless has an entirely different environment. He has always a pace-maker ahead of him and, in his aggressive striving to overtake the older child, may overshoot his mark and become an unobjective rebel. The youngest child may shrink in fear of competing with the more successful older children. The only boy in a family of girls, the only girl in a family of boys, may be discouraged because of this unique position. While no position in the family is without its dangers, it is one of the most important teachings of Individual Psychology, the first science to point out the significance of the ordinal position of the child in the family constellation, that no position can *compel* a child to become neurotic.

Sex in itself may be a factor that complicates the burden of the child. We live in a civilization dominated by a masculine ideal, a civilization that exaggerates masculine values and activities, and still considers, despite good scientific evidence to the contrary, that woman is an inferior sex. The utter fallacy of the prejudice has been exploded by the microscope and the machine, but it exists in widespread tradition nevertheless. Every girl child therefore has an additional burden of proof thrown upon her shoulders. The fact that she is "only a girl" often precludes a normal development along lines of her choice.

The prejudice in favor of the males, however, is not without damage to them. Many a boy is terrified, either by minor physical defects or by other discouraging factors, until he doubts his ability to be a "hundred-per-cent he-man" and spends the rest of his life avoiding the implications and responsibilities of his sex. The increase in marital disharmony, divorce, homosexuality, and sexual delinquency among children, is an important aspect of our overemphasis on sexual differences, and the ever-increasing struggle for prestige that marks the contemporary life of the sexes.

As we have indicated in an earlier section, the normal course of human development may be divided into two phases; an earlier phase of individuation, with growth of the individual at the expense of the environment; and a secondary phase of communal adjustment, marked by the continuation of individuation in terms of social contribution. A child does not grow naturally into the second phase without a certain reconciliation with his adult environment and without a proper initiation into the fellowship of mankind. This initiation is usually accomplished by the intermediation of the child's mother.

A child's mother is the first person with whom the child makes a social contact. Mother's love is the first social approval. As soon as a child realizes that he is appreciated by one other human being he has begun the process of social adjustment. In his mother, and she need not be his blood mother, he experiences the first wholly trustworthy individual in his environment, and with this beginning he can continue his progress toward the normal goal of human adjustment.

It is apparent that the mother has a double function, whose first phase is the reconciliation of the child to his situation in the world, whose second phase consists in encouragement of the child to develop his own powers of growth and adjustment to other individuals. This delicate rôle is seldom played to perfection, and in the mistakes of a child's mother the infinite variety of human patterns may take their origin. There are several typical mistakes, all of which produce easily recognizable types of "problem" adults.

Although children are no longer treated so brutally as they have been in the past, there are nevertheless many mothers in this selfish age who either neglect their children or actually hate them. Illegitimate, ugly, unwanted children often develop antisocial character traits because their guardians have not interested or reconciled them with the world in which they live. It is not strange that many criminals are recruited from the poorer sections of the population, where such neglect and such hate, together with the poverty that leads to ugliness and disease, flourish most widely. These children learn courage and independence in the gutter, but their courage is always the false courage of rebellion against society.

These children can hardly be held entirely responsible for their criminal behavior, so long as society allows them to grow up without the warmth of a mother's love and without the opportunities to develop their social feeling and their sense of social significance. These are the children who feel as if they were hated spies in an enemy land, uncomprehending young aliens in our midst. The prevailing social structure, which vouchsafes opportunities to some and denies them to others, seems to them a greedy dragon, against which they may justifiably take up arms.

A far more common type is the spoiled and pampered and solicitously coddled child who basks in the tropic warmth of a fostering but psychically murderous mother-love throughout the first years of his life. More mothers overdo than underdo their first function of reconciliation. They prove themselves so indispensable to the child that the child never develops the ability to think and act for himself. Such a warm initiation into human society might be very desirable if the child were to live forever like a fairy prince or princess. Unfortunately, this is not the case. Our civilization demands a maximum of contribution, a maximum of adjustment. Its rewards are few, its punishment quick to those who do not pay their dividend of socially useful work in return for the opportunities which civilization guarantees them as individuals.

In some respects the pampered child assumes an attitude toward the world of men almost identical with that of the hated child. He too is an enemy alien, one who was met by a fanfare of trumpets, beautiful speeches, floral tributes, and the keys to the city of the world, so to speak, only to be betrayed as he grows older, only to realize that his cordial reception bears no relation to the tasks before him. Pampering, oversolicitude, overprotection, are false techniques for parents to follow, because they are poor preparation for the communal tasks that the individual child must face later in life. Naturally both hating a child and pampering a child increase his sense of inferiority and complicate his future adjustment. Perhaps in our modern civilization this emotional overemphasis of the child's helplessness is the most potent cause of mistaken patterns of life.

Patterns of life are usually fixed by the time a child is five or six years old. That is to say, a definite set of situations, giving a specific and characteristically individual tinge to the inferiority situation of each child, expresses itself in a characteristic goal in life, which is often crystallized in a phrase-formula. Unless the individual gains insight by later education or by an abrupt change of conditions, this pattern of conduct—between the first inferiority situation and the final crystallized goal of what seems security, totality, superiority—continues as an unchanging dynamic, unified stream.

It is only rarely that an individual learns from his experiences. One can learn from experiences, that is to say, change one's pattern, only if one has previously learned the art of being objective about oneself. This art is seldom learned spontaneously—it derives usually from some external influence or education. The great majority of human beings make their experiences fit into their patterns. Unconsciously they so live that the appropriate experiences occur. After a fashion our experiences are predestined by the nature of our childhood inferiority situation and its fictional compensation in the consequent goal of life. Only that individual who has learned to understand completely the pattern of his own life, who can change his goal if necessary, who realizes the bad and the good in his own conduct, can be said to be the master of his own fate and the captain of his own soul. It is the outstanding merit of Individual Psychology that its study helps us to understand our own goals and our own patterns, and to change them, at least to the extent that lesser errors are substituted for the major mistakes of neurotic conduct.

Once the goal of superiority has been crystallized, each individual proceeds toward its attainment as directly as the obstacles of reality permit. Toward this end each one of us chooses a kit of appropriate tools and a scale of appropriate values. We call these tools character traits, and the whole kit, the personality. A human personality may be considered the sum total of the instruments and devices which any individual has chosen to attain his life goal. The theory of the "splitting of the personality" so commonly used in other systems of psychology becomes only a fiction which describes certain psychic phenomena but does not explain them. The personality is a unity as we explained in the beginning of this essay, and what seems to be a "splitting of the personality" is no more than the choice of a different set of tools to meet a different situation. It would be ludicrous to hold that a stockbroker who played "bull" on the market one day, and "bear" the next was suffering from a dissociation of personality. His goal, and his pattern remain the same: to make money. Only the instruments have changed!

The characteristic instruments which an individual chooses vary with his physical constitution, his environment, the age in which he lives, and the resistance he meets. Thus we have patterns of life as different as the aggressiveness of the "go-getter" and the submission of the saint. Mussolini and Mahatma Gandhi may be striving for the identical goal—time and environment force them to choose unrelated means. In the case of children the pattern of life is often dictated by the special interests of the parents. It is not fortuitous that preachers' sons are frequently sinners, that lawyers' and policemen's sons are often criminals; a protesting child who feels overpowered by the artificial authority of an overbearing parent is quick to search out the psychological weaknesses of that parent and strike at the Achilles' heel of the parent's pattern. Specially well-developed talents in an older brother may lead to the choice of another sphere of activity in a younger brother who fears to compete in the same field. If one child follows the model of the father, a second child, contesting with the first for the family prestige, is almost compelled to choose the mother as an ideal, and in deprecating the model of the first child develop his sense of security and totality along the only path that remains to him.

In this way each individual builds up a scheme of apperception with which he tests all his experiences. It is this artificially developed scale of values which he applies to every experience that he meets. The fable of Procrustes and his ill-famed bed is the nearest analogy to this scheme of apperception. Just as Procrustes stretched unfortunate visitors who were too short for his bed until they met its proportions, and lopped off the feet of those who were too long for it, so each individual subjects every experience to the Procrustean bed of his apperception formula. In this we find an explanation of the diverse consequences of the same experience to a number of individuals. To use another analogy, we have the Great War making brutes out of some, shell-shocked neurotics out of others, ardent and active workers for world-peace of still others, while some because of the nature of their life pattern remain entirely untouched by their experience.

### THE ORIGIN OF PSYCHOPATHOLOGY IN THE INDIVIDUAL

Individual Psychology is a relative and comparative science, not a normative body of laws. There is no categoric imperative, no panacea for all ills, no simple formula for personal salvation. Yet it is desirable to outline a *relative* norm, appropriate to our times, with which we can compare the behavior of those whom we call neurotics, criminals, and psychotics. If we were to dare to outline a normal it would be the pattern of an individual whose goal in life was to be a complete human being, compensating for his personal weaknesses and the experiences of his childhood by some socially valuable, productive work. Such a human being would develop the traits of honesty, sincerity, responsibility. As he grew older his social connections would become more extended, his usefulness wider, his poise better, his courage greater. He would be independent in action and judgment and service, but his activities would be dominated by the social need of his time. What vanity and ambition were left unresolved in his struggle for significance would be impressed into his technique of contributing to the commonweal. He would regard members of the opposite sex as honored fellow workers and equitably divide not only the labors but the prerogatives of life with them.

Even in such bald outline it becomes apparent that most human beings deviate widely from this norm. Only a few human beings make humanity and humanism their goal in life. Many could formulate their goal in life in such phrases as "I want to be godlike" or "I must be the center of all human attention," "I must be beloved by all," "I must sexually conquer all women (or men) to be happy," "I wish to be a one-hundred-per-cent male," "I want all the happiness I can get with the least expenditure of energy," "I must protect myself from the machinations of my evil fellow men," "I must avoid all responsibility and return to the childhood paradise of my youth," "I want to be a baby all my life," "I must dominate my environment by my knowledge," "I must be sick all my life so that society will take care of me," or "I must avoid all risks." These and a thousand similar goals in life are the results of mistaken evaluations of the childhood situation. The more inferior a child feels himself in the beginning, the higher his goal of compensatory superiority, the closer to the idea of godlikeness. The sick child wants to be entirely healthy, the poor child rich, the myopic child wants to translate the world into visual values, the clumsy child desires complete dexterity, the hated child demands a "plus" of love beyond the gifts of mankind. The goal of impotence is omnipotence. As the individual's goal is set long before he realizes that power and security come with growth and development, this goal is frequently beyond the reach of human aspiration and activity.

Now and again in the course of human existence an individual finds a technique which gives him a *subjective* sense of having attained his goal. It may then happen that the technique is elevated into a secondary goal. The phenomenon of the preponderance of the means over the end may then supervene. In this case the individual loses sight of his original goal, and continues the rest of his life in a fatuous repetition and enlargement of his favorite instrument, to the detriment of his efficiency as a human being. For example, a spoiled child who senses that he has lost the paradise of his mother's love, whose goal in life for the first years of his existence is to be an irresponsible pampered baby, is taken sick with a dangerous disease, which brings his parents to his side with their old solicitude and attention. The experience teaches him the value of sickness as a means to power and as a path to the attainment of his ideal. He makes a secondary goal of illness, and approaches each new task, decision, difficulty, or obstacle with one and the same device—illness.

The tragedy of this technique of elevating an instrument (and frequently it is an unworthy tool) into a goal of life, is that the individual loses the normal opportunities to develop the real powers within himself, which might have vouchsafed an objective security. The pragmatic effectiveness is dangerous because such a man knows that the subjective security he has gained by the cult of ill health is false, and he is tortured by his inner need to redouble his efforts and reiterate his ill health, until, sunk in the morass of hypochondriacal self-pity, he not only loses all contact with the world, and all sense of real values, but his joy in living as well. The tragedy of the neurosis is that every neurotic eventually pays more dearly for avoiding the responsibilities of living than he would pay for living responsibly. The neurotic lives in unremitting fear that his unconscious devices will be discovered. He fears living, and he fears death. He becomes a living corpse, afraid of being afraid.

A man with a broken leg needs no justification for not running a race, but a neurotic must spend his life justifying his lack of interest in his fellows, his irresponsibility, failure of achievement, his indecision, his procrastinations, his overcautiousness, his sexual perversions, his vanity, his ambition, or his self-pity. Something there is in every human being that recognizes the necessity of being human, of contributing and cooperating in human society. Some call it conscience, some call it the over-soul. Its name is unimportant, but its existence is attested by the continuous efforts of neurotics to justify their failures. Every neurosis is the substitution of an artificially (usually unconsciously) manufactured and arranged "I cannot" for an innate "I will not." To say "I will not" would evoke the criticism of society. "I cannot" not only justifies the neurotic but shifts the onus of his failing to the group, while a subjective sense of justification and exoneration accrues to the neurotic. A neurosis is a self-deceptive device in which a painful alibi is substituted for a useful performance.

The neuroses of adults begin as the "problems" of childhood. Every "problem" child is a potential neurotic. But "problem" children can grow only in "problem" environments. They are, so to speak, the normal reactions to a vicious environment. They flourish best where ignorance of human nature appears most crassly. The whole problem of mental hygiene is a problem in education, a problem which Alfred Adler has courageously attacked by applying his methods to the prevention of conduct deviations in children. This is the great contribution of Adler to contemporary society: other psychiatrists have realized that the neuroses begin in childhood—Adler has developed a technique, not only of investigating these childhood deviations of conduct, but of obviating them. Individual Psychology, therefore, has grown beyond its original scope as a system of psychotherapy, and has taken its place as a fundamental cornerstone of sociology and pedagogy.

When and where do childhood neuroses begin? We may consider a neurosis to be the frustration product of a false pattern of life. In other words, where an individual, having misinterpreted his inferiority situation, and having set out in an unconscious pattern of overcompensation that outrages the laws of reality, objectivity, and communal living, meets with an insuperable obstacle in reality, he produces a new pattern. This new pattern is his neurosis. It represents an attempt either to justify his failure to solve the problem, or to make a psychic detour around it; in some cases he produces a pattern in which the very existence of the obstacle is denied by the creation of a system of hallucinations. The neurosis, furthermore, may represent an attempt to restore a former situation in which problems and obstacles did not exist, or it may take the form of retaliation against those individuals in the immediate environment whom the individual holds responsible for his failure.

A few examples of neuroses in childhood will help us understand their dynamics. An only child, pampered and carefully guarded throughout the first six years of his life, which were marked by difficulties in his digestion, is faced with the task of adjusting himself to the community of the kindergarten for the first time. Naturally his former life is the worst possible preparation for such an adjustment. The kindergarten is the first frustration of his pattern of dominating his environment. Formerly, when his adult environment did not meet his approval he countered with a hunger-strike, which immediately brought his parents to their knees. The hunger-strike was the forerunner of his neurosis, because the child was misusing an organic inferiority to voice his protest against his parents, and club them into submission. We might expect that this child, faced with the seemingly insuperable problem of becoming an ordinary member of a community of twenty children, will counter with similar protests in terms of his digestive "organ dialect." He does this by vomiting every morning on the steps of the school. In the moment that we investigate this behavior in terms of origin, goal, and means to an end, it becomes understandable. The child wants to restore his former favorable situation by making adjustment to the kindergarten impossible.

A first-born son is followed by a sister, who, because of her greater beauty and the willingness to ingratiate herself, displaces him in the family's affection. The boy does not understand the situation, but he considers himself dethroned and displaced by a girl, and betrayed by his mother, who formerly held him more warmly in her affections. Little by little this boy's mistaken goal in life becomes formulated in the phrase: "You must be careful with women. They are false. Consider every woman your enemy!" During the years of childhood and adolescence he pursues this unconscious goal by cruelly teasing all girls, by deprecating everything feminine, by refusing to work for women teachers, by overemphasizing his masculinity. His Procrustes formula becomes crystallized in the dialectic, "Male = good; female = bad." By the time he has reached adolescence he has built up an elaborate system of false evaluations of women and their rôle in life.

The development of sexual maturity presents a new problem. The neurosis may now take one of several directions. If he comes under the influence of some kindly male teacher, or finds some friend who gives him the comfort and communal feeling which he failed to find in his relations with women, he may well choose the neurosis we call homosexuality. In this case he will divert all his love to men, because the problem of loving a woman, marrying, and forming a true human bond, seems impossible in the light of his misconceptions. From this point he begins training himself to be a homosexual by avoiding all relations with women, reading books which glorify friendship between men, and other books which treat of the perfidy of women. He does not realize that these books have been written by other disappointed men who are attempting to justify their own failures.

On the other hand he may consider his sexual maturity as another instrument to effect his domination over women, and he may become a veritable Don Juan, to whom every woman is a challenge to prove his sexual superiority. As a necessary part of the latter pattern he may feel that sexual intercourse is equivalent to subjugation of his partner, and again no real happiness will be possible for him in his relation with women. Such men are interested only in the chase—not in the community of marriage.

Let us take the case of a youngest child in a large family of successful and well-adjusted children. Terrified by the thought of competing with his older brothers and sisters, this child builds another world of fantasy and dream for himself, to substitute for the world of reality, which seems too difficult. He is afraid to make human contacts with other boys and girls, because he feels his inadequacy too deeply. He builds up a new world of fairy tales, a private language, an individual system of values and ideals. Not being able to make contacts with other children, he imagines fantastic companions within himself. He cannot talk the language of others, and therefore develops a language of his own. The fiction of dissociation of personality is necessary to such a child, because no human being can live entirely alone, and it follows, as the night the day, that if the child cannot make contact with other children, he will create imaginary companions, who proffer no risk, who accede to all demands, who fit into the picture of his ideal world.

When this child meets with the real problems of the school, or when he finds his struggle for significance complicated by the strains and stresses of adolescence or disease, it is not surprising that he should develop a pattern of isolation, of negativism, of a cramped relation to the outside world, on the one hand, and on the other, a full inner life. Some of these children gradually reconcile themselves to life, become poets, dreamers, dramatists, writers, occasionally philosophers and psychologists. But it is more than likely, especially if their problems are complicated by certain obscure physical inadequacies of constitution, that they will join the great army which fills our state hospitals with cases of dementia præcox.

The descriptions of schizophrenia, the splittings of the personality, the mutism, the individual language, the negativism, the sexual aberration that all authors have described in this interesting syndrome, can be understood by any student of human nature who sees in all these manifestations the common denominator of hopelessness. As soon as physicians learn to understand the utter logic of the behavior of cases of dementia præcox, their inexorable march toward a goal of isolation and irresponsibility, the fiction that it is always an incurable disease will be dispelled. Many cases of dementia præcox, as Adler has shown, are curable if the physician who treats them is more hopeful than the patient. To accede in the patient's hopelessness, to act "as if" the patient were correct in his deductions, is to produce the very condition that is premised.

### THE HUMAN SITUATION AND THE CHALLENGE OF LIFE

It is impossible to sketch the variety of human patterns of life even in the baldest outline, but it is possible to diagram the situation of every human being in relation to the problems which he must meet. Because of man's relation to the cosmos there are three great groups of problems which he must face. These problems are the problems of society, of work, and of sex.

The first group of problems derive from the biologic necessity of man's communal life. Everyone who wishes to be human must affirm his connection to his fellow men by affirming certain common bonds, notably those of speech, reason, common sense, sympathy, and the like. Society exists for the benefit of the individual. It is the very best means that could be devised to guarantee the full development of the individual's native faculties and powers. The second problem, that of work, arises from the corollarial necessity that each individual uphold the social structure. The individual must pay a dividend to society, and that dividend we call useful work. The third problem derives from the bisexuality of the human race, and from the fact that it may best be solved in these social terms we call love and marriage. The outer forms of love and marriage vary with time and place, but wherever and whenever they occur they always bear a definite relation to the social good of the community.

These three problems may well be compared to a huge three-ring circus in which each and every one of us must play his rôle. The solution of these problems is not a private matter, left to the discretion of each individual. Human society can exist solely by the mutually protective reciprocal contributions of group and individual. As in any other circus, however, there are a variety of side-shows included under the big tent we call the cosmos. Some are nearer to, others farther from the main arena. Anyone who observes the human comedy will find many human beings busily engaged in these side-shows. Their activity seems more feverish than the activity of those performers who go through their paces in the three great rings. These side-show performers are the neurotics and psychotics whose hyperactivity is designed to deceive themselves and their fellow men. They demonstrate their good will, their entire helplessness, their irresponsibility, their extreme activity, as a justification for their desertion from the main arenas.

It must not be believed that these side-show performers are maliciously avoiding their obligations as human beings. It is their ignorance of the coherence of all human activities that enables them to continue patterns whose constant common denominator is social uselessness. They look longingly at the greater arenas of life, for whose challenge they are unprepared, and attempt to exonerate their failures to conform. One hears the phrases: "I would, *if* . . ." and "I know, *but*. . . ." And their entire neurosis is expressed in the "if" and the "but." They make reservations, they make conditions which are impossible of fulfilment, shrug their shoulders, and allow their fellows to assume the responsibility of maintaining them.

The first stages of a neurosis are ushered in by a group of symptoms that constitute what Adler has called "the hesitating attitude." Doubt, indecision, procrastination, pessimism, deprecation of life, anxiety, overcautiousness, exaggerated ambition (which is always ambition for personal power or dominance), isolation, disinterestedness, abnormal fatigue, impatience, and a host of similar character traits mark this hesitating attitude. When we remember that all human activities are purposive, we can deduce what the goal of these traits is. Doubt, vacillation, laziness, are not to be considered static descriptions of character. These are actually very dynamic instruments exquisitely appropriate to their goal: to avoid the final tests of life, to approach problems so slowly that no solution is possible, to maintain what Adler has called "distance" from the normal activities of man. While the boundaries of normalcy and neurosis overlap and are indistinguishable, the degree of this "distance" from the normal goals and activities of human beings is the sole criterion of the severity of the neurosis.

A large proportion of mankind solves the problem of work to a greater or lesser degree because of the tyranny of its stomach. The side-shows about this arena are nevertheless numerous. Individuals, such as beggars, who live on a false exploitation of the sympathy of their fellows, are surely to be considered as side-show artists. Pimps and prostitutes who distort their sexual functions for economic grounds fall in a similar category. "Confidence" men, criminals, and the whole host of underworld characters who live by their wits at the expense of a gullible humanity are individuals who have never realized that work is not a curse, but a form of personal salvation. Those who change from one job to another, not holding to any one piece of work long enough to contribute anything, those who cannot adjust themselves to normal working conditions, those whose work is the exploitation of other human beings, are unhappy men and women who have not understood the meaning and value of work. Women who spend their lives in a futile attempt to escape from ennui via unceasing bridge, mah jong, gossip; gamblers who do not trust their own powers and must therefore worship "Luck"; men and women whose work depends on the cupidity and ignorance of their fellows—these crowd the ranks of the vast army which lacks the courage to face the problem of becoming productive, useful contributors to the welfare of mankind.

Isolation is practically impossible in a world growing more and more interrelated and cooperative with every passing day. Only the insane, who completely break the bridge of human contact, ever effectively isolate themselves. As we have previously indicated, the ideal social relation of an individual to the society in which he lives consists in the building of as many bridges to his fellow men as he finds it possible to construct. The only security of which a man can be sure is the security which originates in the good will of his fellow men. Because of the faults of our education many unhappy souls attempt to win this security by building walls around themselves instead of constructing bridges to their fellows. The technique of isolation is the technique of snobbery, of bigotry, of hate, of suspicion, of jealousy, of envy, of egoism in the last analysis. Professional class-consciousness, patrioteering, clannishness, pride, vanity, misanthropy, are tools of the tendency to egotistic seclusion. Discourtesy, pedantic fastidiousness, sullenness, vulgarity, ostentation, make the task of social adjustment more difficult. These are the side-shows of the social life.

Because our training for the sexual problems of our time is relatively unsuited to the development of a normal attitude toward sex, because we still live in a world in which sexual antagonism rather than sexual cooperation is the rule, and because, unlike the other two sets of problems, the solution of the sexual problem is not immediately necessary to individual life, and its good solution demands a high degree of social feeling, the side-shows about this arena are more numerous, perhaps, than those about the other two. A full catalogue, under the circumstances, would lead us beyond the scope of this essay. Suffice it to say that the existence of those major sexual deviations of our times—homosexuality in both men and women, frigidity in women, and impotence in men, dyspareunia in sexual relations, prostitution, sadism and masochism, fetishism, the excesses of "free love," the puritan spirit, the neurotic pruriency of the Watch and Ward Society, the cult of pornography, the inhuman exploitation of sexual problems in the tabloid newspapers, the legal proscription of contraceptive information—is evidence that a very considerable portion of the human race finds itself in the side-shows of the sexual arena. When we add celibacy, masturbation phobias, sexual asceticism, "white slavery," child marriages, incest, both physical and mental (as in the abnormal attachment of parents to children of the opposite sex), rape, and the long list of perverted sexual practices of our time, we realize how little prepared for the sexual problem the average "civilized" man and woman is.

It is not surprising that a certain system of psychology has premised that all human woes begin with sexual maladjustment, and all neuroses are based on aberrations of the sexual function. Students of the Adlerian psychology will quickly see the fallacies underlying such a system of psychology. Sexual behavior is never a cause of neurosis or insanity—it is one of its manifestations. It is frequently the first sign of neurosis, but a careful analysis of the entire pattern of an individual's conduct, an examination of his goal in life, and his technique of approach to his goal, will demonstrate that the neurotic attitude may be found in his social and occupational reactions as well.

### THE THEORY AND PRACTICE OF THERAPY

The therapy of Individual Psychology is based on the application of its philosophic premises. The "cure" of the neurosis depends on the art of giving the neurotic insight into his errors and the demonstration of the inefficiency of his technique together with the encouragement to find better goals and patterns. It means that the psychiatrist discloses the neurotic's hidden and secret goal of domination to him, traces the formation of his unconscious pattern, ferrets out his apperception formula, applies it to the material which the patient presents in his autobiographical data as well as in his present activities and desires, and eventually convinces the neurotic, in the course of friendly conversations, which are carried out without dim lights, couches, or hypnotic suggestions, that more human goals offer him greater human satisfactions than the false securities of his neurosis.

Realizing that the neurotic patient has somewhere falsely interpreted his childhood situation, the Adlerian psychiatrist reenacts the rôle which the neurotic's mother has somehow failed to fulfil. He wins the patient by presenting an attitude of indestructible good will, patience, and sympathy. The patient relives the early inferiority situation only to learn that his inferiority complex is an unnecessary and subjective product of a childhood misconception of the objective state of affairs. Presently he learns that the bulwarks of human friendship are stronger than the spurious walls of isolation.

During the analysis and reeducation of the patient the Adlerian psychiatrist abrogates all personal authority. This is in contradistinction to the methods of psychoanalysis, in which the analyst demands absolute servility, and denies the patient the use of his critical faculties. The Adlerian reeducation is in the nature of a cooperative research between physician and patient, in which the patient contributes the material from his life, the psychiatrist furnishes interpretation and encouragement. The psychiatrist minimizes any personal superiority of insight. Like any good educator he uses his position to encourage, not to humiliate his pupil. Together they work out a new goal, always the goal of active humanism, and a new technique of its attainment suited entirely to the individual's needs. As the analysis of the situation can be sketched, usually, during the first few hours of these conferences, much less time is spent in the fatuous research of details of the dead past, which can offer only further corroboration and affirmation of the pattern, once the pattern has been established, while more time is spent on the synthesis of valuable existing elements into a new and more effective pattern of life.

There can be no place for moralizing in such a research. The psychiatrist holds no moral superiority over his patient. His attitude is always: "Under what circumstances, and toward what goal, would I employ the same technique of living?" Knowing that every neurosis is essentially the product of discouragement, the psychiatrist sets his pupil easy tasks, which are well within the patient's power to solve. In this way the patient—and in the Adlerian psychology the relation of physician and patient is much more the relation of teacher and pupil—enlarges his initial capital of courage and social feeling, only to be given progressively more difficult tasks, until his behavior pattern approaches the normal in all three problems of life. No attempt is made to make a perfect human of the patient. The benefit the patient derives from his newly gained insight is that he is enabled to substitute minor errors for the major mistakes of his neurosis; by living a fuller life, he gains a greater joy in living.

In the treatment of children with behavior and conduct problems the Individual Psychologist finds the Adlerian technique simple and amazingly effective. After reading a case protocol, or hearing a mother's description of her child's difficulties, the psychiatrist has usually gained insight into the nature of the child's specific problem. Problem children have simple patterns, and to those who can read and interpret the signs, the remedies are almost immediately apparent. Problem children, as the case histories given here demonstrate, are those who have been discouraged by any or all of the factors described in the first paragraphs of this foreword. The problem usually lies with the parents, who have frustrated the normal channels of the child's development by the interposition of additional difficulties and obstacles. The treatment of problem children, then, consists largely in the education of parents and teachers to the understanding of the dynamic patterns of the child's conduct and the removal, wherever possible, of discouraging factors.

The logical and trenchant simplicity of Individual Psychology is attested by the fact that children very often understand its workings and may be won over to its point of view. In the case of the very young child the problem is solved by the removal of the discouraging factors by the parents and the psychiatrist. In older children there is a definite training toward courage, toward independence, and toward the acquisition of the social feeling. While Individual Psychology cannot claim to cure all cases of problem behavior in children, even the most difficult cases respond to its treatment when parents and teachers can be taught to cooperate intelligently in the treatment.

Alfred Adler has always claimed that the school was the ideal locus for the prophylactic mental-hygiene clinic. Here every child faces a microcosm of the world in the social situation of the schoolroom and its tasks. Teachers who have learned Adler's method of approach, and his technique of influencing the child mind, find their classroom tasks materially lightened. The recognition of neurotic behavior patterns is the first step in their redirection into normal channels. Children react as surely to encouragement and understanding as plants react to sun and rain and proper soil, and it is quite as easy for parents and teachers to understand and to encourage as it is to put children in static categories and discourage them. The Adlerian psychology posits as a first principle: "Every human being can do everything." This theorem has limitations well known to its discoverers, but as a pragmatic principle in human relations it is invaluable. One thing is certain: when teachers categorize children as bad, as stupid, as lazy, as neurotic, nothing is accomplished thereby but to make them stupid and neurotic. To treat them as such usually results in the child's obliging with the very conduct that is expected of him. To treat a child "as if" he could adjust himself to the scheme of human society costs nothing, and often accomplishes miracles.

This necessarily brief introduction to Individual Psychology is not for pessimists or for cowards; but it is hoped that those readers who believe that human beings have a spark which may be kindled into a steady flame, those readers who believe that human beings have the right to be happy in being human, will find in it the stimulus to continue their studies. The cases cited in the following pages will help them to understand something of the technique of reading the patterns of human life as a skilled musician reads the score of a symphony. Beyond this, Individual Psychology is an art more than a science. Its application is a matter of creative intuition, of that fine empathy with human striving which has actuated great poets and great teachers throughout the history of mankind. None who has not lived life fully and shared profoundly the woes and the ecstasy of living need expect to master the art, yet everyone who is a thinking human being has it in his power to become a good craftsman, capable of mastering and applying its fundamental principles.

W. Béran Wolfe, M.D.
*New York City*

## *A GESTURE OF THE WHOLE BODY*

THIS evening we have the problem of Miss Flora, whose chief complaint is that for years she has been subject to attacks of unconsciousness. She lives with her mother, father, two younger and two older brothers, and two young children. The relationships in the home are very congenial, and the patient, who is the only girl, has always had her own way and has been distinctly favored by the father.

Now when we hear of attacks of unconsciousness we think immediately of epilepsy, but epilepsy is a word that is very loosely used to describe a variety of illnesses. The differential diagnosis is sometimes exceedingly hard to make and is entirely the concern of the physician. Usually people who suffer from epilepsy are facing great difficulties in their lives, and, these difficulties being mirrored in their mental attitude, it is sometimes hard to decide where the organic disease leaves off and its mental superstructure begins. Epilepsy has always been called a sickness, because up to the present time epileptics have been taken care of by physicians. It is rather similar to the attitude of laymen toward the neuroses, which were previously always called hysteria.

There are a number of symptoms that are highly significant in the differential diagnosis between a true epilepsy and a simulated epilepsy. In a real epileptic attack the pupils of the eyes are dilated and do not react to light. This is one of the most important signs of an organic epilepsy. So far nothing like this sign is mentioned in the case history of Flora. The second important symptom is the presence of the Babinski reflex during the fainting spells. To test the Babinski reflex we stroke the sole of the foot and find that the great toe rises (toward the dorsum of the foot) instead of moving downward as one would normally expect. The Babinski reflex signifies that an injury has occurred to a certain part of the brain and this injury prevents the passage of the nervous impulse along its usual routes. There are other symptoms that point to the presence of a true epilepsy. Sometimes one finds small hemorrhages below the skin, especially behind the ear; often the epileptic patient bites his tongue during the attack, and we find that his saliva is bloody. Frequently, too, the epileptic falls and hurts himself during his attack. The epileptic often has a fleeting presentiment that the attack will occur. We call this the aura, which varies in its form but is usually present.

This group of symptoms, which are present in a true epilepsy, distinguishes it from other fainting attacks of an hysterical nature, in which the person feels himself injured, hopeless, and powerless, and expresses his attitude in a gesture of his entire body.

The fainting attack of an hysterical patient means: "I am powerless." The hysterical patient recuperates quickly from his attack, but the true epileptic attack is followed usually by a period of somnolence, headache, and malaise, which may last several hours. One of the important differential points between epilepsy and hysteria is that the epileptic does not know that he has fainted—he realizes it only after the attack is over.

To add to our difficulties in making a differential diagnosis, most cases of epilepsy are associated with certain mental deficiencies. If you attack a true epileptic in such a way that he would normally respond with a fit of anger, you may increase the frequency of his attacks. Epileptic persons often have bad tempers, and in investigating the families of epileptics, I have usually been able to find that one member of the family has a conspicuously bad temper. We must interpret a bad temper as the sign of an inferiority complex, and where I have found epileptic children in a family of an irascible father, I have sometimes felt that they were imitating their father's tantrums.

Sometimes epileptic fits are later complicated by an epileptic insanity, which is usually marked by hallucinations and wild and cruel behavior. Epileptics are usually treated in asylums by the use of sedative drugs, which make them dreamy and sleepy most of the time, and under such treatment the number of epileptic attacks often is decreased although the attacks are not wholly stopped.

In spite of all the differences which exist between true epilepsy and hysterical attacks of unconsciousness, a true diagnosis is hard to make because a doctor is seldom present when the attack occurs to examine the eyes and test the Babinski reflex.

According to my experience, epileptic attacks occur only in certain susceptible people when they are in a bad situation. I believe that this susceptibility consists in a pathologic variation of the blood-vessels of the brain. An epileptic attack much resembles the picture of a man in a towering rage. The epileptic looks as if he wanted to attack somebody. An epilepsy no doubt occurs most frequently in those individuals who have both the pathologic variation of the cerebral blood-vessels and the tendency to have fits of anger. Usually epileptics are very cruel, and in their dreams they often experience brutality and fighting. Cruelty plays a large rôle in the mental make-up of the epileptic, and though you will find apparently very kind, sweet, and quiet individuals who are epileptic, when you investigate their dreams you will find anything but benevolence. There is no doubt that alcohol increases the frequency of epileptic attacks, and this could be proved experimentally if it were not too inhuman. Epileptics who are adversely influenced by alcohol must avoid it in every form.

In my experience with epilepsy I have found that it is advisable to allow the epileptic patient to live as easy a life as possible, and it has been my experience, furthermore, that the patient's situation can be bettered if he is taught to be stronger, more self-reliant and calmer. In other words, I have found that epilepsy disappeared when the patient became socially well adjusted, even in cases where many other physicians had corroborated the diagnosis. I do not mean by this that I am able to cure epilepsy, but I do say that the symptoms of epilepsy can sometimes be alleviated and the patient made much more comfortable if we can bring about a greater degree of social adjustment. And it is certainly true that in some cases where the social adjustment has reached a high level the epileptic symptoms have completely disappeared.

Now let us go on with our case. We have learned that it is that of an only girl in a family of brothers, and it has been my observation that in such a family a girl is overindulged and frequently does not develop her normal feminine rôle. She will often be very obedient, but hardly ever self-confident and independent; and she will develop in such a way that others will always have to support her. More than likely she will be unable to stay alone. On the other hand, there is a different type of development in this situation, when such an only girl develops as if she were a boy, becomes very hardy, and exaggerates her boyish tendencies. The case history must show which of these two paths our patient has followed.

We learn that a congenial relationship exists in the entire family and that the girl has always had her own way and been favored by her father. We may expect, therefore, that our patient will show the characteristics of a pampered child who has not developed sufficient strength of mind. She is probably very sweet, quiet, and obedient, and very greedy for appreciation. I find in the case notes this statement:

> "Since her first attack she sleeps with her mother."

Here is evidence that the girl not only refuses to be alone, but that her first attack served to accentuate her dependence. This point leads me to believe that the so-called epilepsy is premeditated. The notes further state:

> "The family life is very complete. The patient's health has been perfectly normal and there has been no sign indicating a neurosis heretofore. Her mother says that she is almost perfect in every way. She has made friends easily."

The mother's remark about Flora's perfection corroborates my belief that she belongs to the first type, and is a sweet, obedient young woman. It is also quite certain that she is a spoiled child and it is high time she should be made independent. Such independence would be of great advantage to her; it is, in fact, her only hope of a cure.

> "Her recreations are the movies, theater, and riding in the auto. She did excellent work in school

and graduated fourth in her class. She worked after school, and enjoyed her work."

Her school record perhaps shows that she wanted to be a favorite in school as well as in the home and did good work in order to be properly appreciated.

"At present she is occupied as a secretary and says she likes her work. While she was at school she wanted to be a teacher, but gave up her ambition because of the extra effort that was required."

Here again we see that she lacks self-confidence and will make no effort to become independent.

"The patient is now twenty-five years old, is said to be good-looking, although she has a slight cast in one eye. She has one joint of her engagement-ring finger cut off, but she holds her hand in such a way that this is seldom noticed."

Undoubtedly these defects have played an important rôle in her life, and she tries to protect herself from their consequences. She approaches life with a hesitating attitude, as if she did not trust herself very far.

"It is impossible to get any early memories from her, and she complains it is hard for her to recall her youth."

I believe that if I had tried to get her childhood recollections she would have been able to remember.

Some people have difficulty in recalling childhood experiences because they believe they must recall some horrible episode before their twelfth or thirteenth year. This is not at all necessary. I usually ask, "Do you remember your school-days?" The patient frequently feels very cautious about answering this. The choice of a patient's recollections is an important clue to his personality. After some of the school incidents are recalled the patient often remembers certain pre-school experiences. I sometimes advise my patients to write all that they can remember about their early childhood, as if they were making notes for an autobiography. This patient recalls two dreams, however, which it may be of interest to hear.

> "'I dreamed of having a petting party with a boy who works in the drugstore where I take lunch. I also had the same dream about my boss.'"

This dream again shows us that our patient wants to be petted and made much of, not only at home but also where she works. If her employer did pamper her she would probably not dream about it, and so we may conclude that he is not so kind to her as she would like. She creates the situation in a dream: "How would it be if he petted me? How can I make him love me?" You see she is preparing the way to her goal, and that is to be loved. This much certainly we can interpret in the dream. The boy in the drugstore has probably not had a petting party with her. We may conclude that she is not in the position in which she would like to be, which is an important factor in our interpretation.

> " 'I dreamed that a tide was overtaking the other people on the street. It did not touch me, and I just looked on.' "

Now this second dream is much more significant because it shows the patient's innate cruelty, as she sees other people drowning without offering help. This dream means: "How could I create a situation in which the other people in the world would drown and I would be alone? How would it feel to be wholly alone?" Very probably she would like to save her father and mother from the deluge, but she is not interested in other people, she would let them drown. Why should she want everyone else to perish? We can safely conclude that she hates the rest of the world because she feels powerless to make them love her. The only way to remedy the situation is to extinguish the whole of mankind. This idea suggests a superiority complex, but we know that a superiority is always based on an inferiority complex. Her dream is like an outburst of temper. It is as if she said, "Let the people perish!"

> "She complains that her mother does not make the grandchildren mind, but that she can make the children, who are five and seven, obey her."

This gives us an indication of why she wanted to be a teacher. She believes that a teacher is always surrounded by obedient children, and she wants them to show their appreciation of her by obedience.

> "She believes that the family have been too good to her and too easy with her."

This report shows that she has a considerable insight into her own situation, but nothing is changed by such a statement, except that it is valuable for appearances' sake. We know that what she wants is to have everybody in submission to her, her employer, the drugstore clerk, the children, and her parents. Her problem is how to reach this goal. Otherwise her entire scheme of life is shattered and she is powerless.

> "The first attack of epilepsy occurred after she had been working some two years in the same office. She screamed and fell to the floor of the office where many people were working. Her head struck the concrete floor, she bit her tongue and had to be held by force until she was removed to her home, where she was attended by several doctors and a trained nurse. She was very ill for a week and at the same time developed kidney poisoning."

This sounds as if the first attack were real epilepsy, but as she had another illness at the same time it is quite possible that her faint was not entirely epileptic. We must reserve our judgment and investigate further.

"The next attack occurred seven months later, when she was in her own home. She fell and burned her arm badly on a curling-iron. Although her aunt was in the house at the time, her mother had gone off on an overnight visit, for the first time since the child was born."

If this is a real case of epilepsy then it certainly has had a very uncommon development. For usually, when epilepsy is diagnosed as late as the eighteenth year, there is a history of minor attacks preceding the major attacks. This case occurred too suddenly. The first attack began at the eighteenth year, and the illness became aggravated to such an extent that the patient had to sleep with her mother. The next attack, coming seven months later, curiously coincides with the fact that her mother was away on an overnight visit for the first time since the child's birth. This is surely remarkable. The unavoidable conclusion is that our patient wants to rule her mother, even though her rule is expressed in a sweet, kind manner. The attack is one way of saying, "Why did you leave me alone?" You see we must learn to understand the language of the entire body.

Thirteen months passed before the next attack. During this time the patient took luminal and was on a diet. Patients are usually rather weak as a consequence of the diet and the luminal, but the treatment helps to tide the patient over, and sometimes has good effect.

> "After the last attack, the attacks of unconsciousness have come every month at the time of the menstrual period. The attacks are most violent at this time. At present they occur almost every week and are ushered in by the patient's calling her mother when she feels the attack coming."

These are important clues to the nature of the illness. The beginning of menstruation was a period of great difficulty for this girl. She had an attack of unconsciousness at the beginning of menstruation, which was probably due to her desire not to admit she was actually a girl instead of a boy, as she would prefer. Whenever the menstrual period arrives the patient becomes more tense, and it is this tension which is an important determinant of the beginning of the spells. That she calls her mother when she feels the attack coming, further indicates its purpose. The case history says, "At one time she felt one coming and went outdoors where there were neighbors near by." This shows that she wanted someone to replace her mother when she was absent.

> "Her intelligence decreases during the epileptic fits and her attacks often occur after she has had a quarrel."

I do not know what we can do to help this patient, but our treatment will be directed toward changing her entire style of living, and reconciling her with her female rôle. At this point it would be wise to consider her relations to her lover, since she dislikes being a woman. Although I have not read the entire history, I feel sure that we shall find some expression of the inferiority complex in her love life. We shall have to ask her lover the details, but perhaps the case notes will help us.

> "She has been going with the same boy for eight years. She has been engaged for three years. She notices that the attacks have been more frequent since her engagement."

I think we will all agree that going with one boy for eight years is too long. And since her attacks are more frequent now, I am sure that one of two things will happen. Either her fiancé will be shocked by her illness and decide not to marry her, or she will insist on the formula, "Wait until I am well." These attacks will help her maintain her formula. It is her goal in life to avoid the female rôle and defer any decision about marriage. She fears that she will be ruled by men, and she has assumed her formula, "Wait until I am well," as a last line of defense. She wants to escape, to hesitate.

> "There is another boy on the scene at present. She loves the second boy, but feels that she must be true to the one who has waited so long. The first boy knows nothing of his rival, and says he wants to wait until Flora is well. She says, 'I would marry if I did not have these attacks.' "

Now it is a rule that two boys are less than one, and we can understand how being in love with two men defers the question of marrying one of them. Her goal in life is to escape the problem of love and she realizes her goal, not only by dividing her love interests, but by exaggerating her fainting spells to demonstrate that she is not responsible. But you must not believe that these actions are conscious or malicious. The girl is sick, and it is a part of her pattern of life to be unconscious of the real meaning of her attacks. You see how appropriate this pattern is for the attainment of her hidden goal. The fact that she wants to be true to the boy who has waited so long, is perhaps a sign of her scrupulous conscience, but what we must do in the treatment is to show her that she is not as conscientious as she believes. I am a little suspicious of the boy who says he will wait until she is well, and perhaps she has chosen him as a lover because he falls in with her plans and is willing to wait. It is interesting to see how she formulates her own style of life in the statement, "I would marry, if I did not have these attacks." This demonstrates her good will, to be sure, but the real meaning of the statement can be derived solely from the dramatic aside which we do not hear: "But I do have them!"

The case history gives two more important points.

"At the time of the second attack a grandchild was born and Flora's mother kept her at the house most of the time. Also at this time she met the first young man with whom she fell in love."

This second attack is very questionable and it is probable that Flora unconsciously realized she could achieve much more in the house if she were ill.

### Conference

Flora enters the room.

Dr. Adler. I should like to ask whether you had a good position when you were taken sick? Were you having any difficulties in the office?

Flora. I had considered leaving the position several times. I was not happy in the place because there were too many people and too much excitement.

Dr. Adler. Did you like your employer and the people you worked with?

Flora. Yes, my companions were very nice and my employer was typical of most employers.

Dr. Adler. I understand that you had some kidney trouble and this might have made working difficult for you. Did your employer ever criticize you?

Flora. No, he never criticized me. I was perfectly well.

Dr. Adler. But you wanted to leave your job.

Flora. Yes.

Dr. Adler. Are you working now?

Flora. Yes, as a secretary in a real estate office.

Dr. Adler. Do you like your new job?

FLORA. Yes, I like it very much better.

DR. ADLER. I am glad that you have bettered your position. Can you tell me something that you remember from your early childhood? It need not be anything very important. Perhaps you can remember what you liked and what you disliked.

FLORA. That's rather hard to say. I suppose I liked outdoor sports.

DR. ADLER. Which sports did you like best?

FLORA. Skating, sliding down hill, and climbing trees.

DR. ADLER. You must have been a very brave girl.

FLORA. I had to be. I had four brothers to contend with.

DR. ADLER. Were you able to stand it?

FLORA. I think I always held my own.

DR. ADLER. Do you remember wishing you were a boy?

FLORA. No, I don't think I ever wanted to be a boy, but I always played with boys because there were no girls to associate with.

DR. ADLER. I suppose you were brought up like a boy, and had many boy friends because of your brothers.

FLORA. Undoubtedly.

DR. ADLER. I think if you speak with your teacher who has brought in the history, she will tell you why you have become so very sensitive. You are a person who easily gets in a state of great tension, and you have these fainting spells to demonstrate your weakness. They occur only when you have been crossed or criticized. It seems to me you are a little afraid of the future, and that you do not trust yourself enough. I think also that you do not want to decide things for yourself and that you want to be loved without any effort on your part. I can understand such a state of mind very well; but I believe that your health will be improved if you are more courageous and if you realize that you need not always contend with your brothers. There are better ways to live than always being in a position of complete powerlessness. Wouldn't you like to try another way?

FLORA. Yes, of course.

DR. ADLER. The whole trouble is that you are not brave enough. I would suggest that you decide to assume the whole responsibility for your own actions, and I am sure that if you take this one step it will be tremendously helpful to you.

FLORA. Do you mean that if I am courageous I can cure my attacks?

DR. ADLER. Yes.

FLORA. Well, I am willing to try anything.

## *MATERNAL DOMINATION*

THIS evening we are to consider the case of Robert, who is eleven years and eight months old. There is some doubt in the mind of his teacher as to whether or not the boy is feeble-minded. The problem of feeble-mindedness is extremely difficult and complicated, and we must be very careful in our diagnosis, because the patient's failure or success as a human being may depend entirely upon our decision.

It is reasonable to expect a completely normal boy of this age to have reached at least the fifth grade, but the case notes state:

> "The boy is retarded in school; he is in the third grade, and has a very low intelligence quotient. He is quiet and docile in his class. In the past he has always been slow and timid and did not learn to speak until very late."

It seems as if there were really a considerable retardation in this case, but sometimes normal children also are slow and timid, especially if they are left-handed. Frequently the left-handed child is not clever with his hands and, having experienced a number of defeats and failures, he expresses his overcautiousness by slow movement. The fact that this boy did not learn to talk until very late is suspicious, because we know that this is a common difficulty with feeble-minded children. Where the mental defect is profound they do not learn to speak at all. On the other hand, there is also a certain type of spoiled child who does not talk until late. We have a special word for this type in German, but there is no such word in English. These children can hear, but do not speak, although they are not deaf and dumb. Under such circumstances it is very hard to determine whether a child is or is not feeble-minded, especially as some of these children prove later to be intelligent, and good talkers. I know of some people, both among the dead and among the living, who, after great difficulty in the beginning, were able to speak beautifully later in life. In this case we must look for one of two patterns—either that of a feeble-minded child, or that of a spoiled child. In some respects the patterns of the spoiled child and the feeble-minded child are identical. It is possible that this child is a combination of both and we may have some difficulty in deciding what the truth is.

> "The father is a short, stout, retiring man, the mother a charming and attractive woman. There are two older sisters, sixteen and fourteen years old; there have not been any other children. The parents are congenial; there are no quarrels, but the mother dominates the home. The mother

> says that the father favors the elder girl but that the boy has been closer to her."

You see that he has a certain advantage in being the only boy and the baby of the family. Perhaps it is a contradiction, but I have not seen many happy marriages in which one parent or the other dominated the home. When the mother says that the boy is closer to her, she does not express herself very fully. She probably might add, "I have spoiled him."

> "The boy speaks oftener of his mother than of other members of the family. The family calls him Buster, a very inappropriate nickname because he is slow and retarded. Both girls are in high school and are very bright."

When one child in the family is very bright we can usually look for difficulties with the other children. The superiority of the more intelligent child makes the other children appear inferior by contrast, and this probably has happened in the case under consideration. An over-petted child is easily discouraged, and it may be that this is the trouble with Robert. This gives us a little hope, because it is easier to discourage an intelligent child than a feeble-minded boy, and allows us to conclude that the child had more courage before he went to school. Perhaps, after all, it is not a case of feeble-mindedness.

"Entrance to school is gained by a competitive examination, and the record of his two sisters was held up to the boy. His present teacher has discouraged this."

This corroborates our point very satisfactorily.

"The father takes a negative attitude toward the child. He believes that the boy was born this way and will always be this way. The mother says that none of the children were ever spanked. She says, 'He is our only boy, the baby, and it was such a blow to find that he was not like the others.' "

The father's hopelessness is discouraging, because very often a child develops according to his father's opinion of him. On this account particularly, it will be our duty to encourage the child and let him feel that there is hope for his normal development. The fact that the child has progressed as far as the third grade in the public school leads me to believe that this is not a hopeless case.

Suppose we try thinking of Robert as if he were only a problem child, leaving the question of his feeble-mindedness entirely out of consideration. We find that his position in the family has been very circumscribed: on the one hand, he is too closely connected with his mother and dependent on her for support; on the other hand, he cannot compete with the two older girls, who are brighter than he is. As he is not courageous, he does not fight—he remains quiet, as we have heard. We can hardly expect that such a boy would develop very well. You might compare it, for instance, with three trees growing in a narrow place—if two of the trees have overcome the difficulties and grown strong, the third tree cannot grow freely. The same thing holds true for children. In this family the girls have taken up all the available space, and the boy has been forced to place his goal on the lower level: not to go on. In this way we can explain his entire pattern of development.

> "The girls are very companionable with each other. The boy speaks oftener of the older girl, who takes him for walks and to the movies. He claims the younger girl teases him, and he teases her in retaliation."

The younger girl and the boy show the extremes of the situation. The younger girl is active and aggressive, and although there is not much said about her it is almost certain that she is striving to be the first in the family; whereas the boy, having been discouraged, has given up his efforts and is content to remain in the rear. The fact that the boy and the younger girl tease each other bespeaks their competition. She is fourteen years old and he is nearly twelve. This means that she was two and a half years old when he was born. She felt herself dethroned by his presence, and her attack was directed against him so successfully that he did not try to compete.

> "The family's finances are fair. The mother keeps house, while the father manages a local grocery, in which he has a financial interest. The girls are well dressed and do not work in their spare time. There are five rooms, and five single beds; each member of the family sleeps alone. The boy sleeps with his face to the wall and sometimes curls up."

I have done some research in this matter of sleep-attitudes, and I have found that a great deal may be discovered by watching the way people sleep at night. The boy's sleep-attitude seems to say, "I am not courageous. I do not want to see anything." When he curls up, it means that he would like to disappear, or roll himself into a ball like a hedgehog, so as to offer no exposure to the enemy.

> "The father sleeps in the same room with the boy, and the mother says that she must sometimes lie down with the boy and quiet him until he falls asleep."

This latter point is important because it shows that the boy is very fearful and demands that his mother support him in his timidity. He does not want to function as an independent being, and regulates his behavior to compel his mother's attention. Put this boy in a situation where he is not with her, such as a classroom at school, and he is discouraged. In a way, he turns his back and closes his eyes in a fashion symbolized by his sleep-attitude. It is evident that he does not want to be confronted by any problems.

> "The mother admits that she slept with the boy until he was much older than the other children. The parents are of Italian descent, but there are no limitations placed by the father on the mother and the girls, as is common in some Italian families. The mother says, 'I have full control at home. Sometimes my husband tells me I ought not to go out, as I am too tired, because like all men he does not want me to go out, but he does not say so in so many words.' "

The mother's admission proves that Robert has been humored more than his sisters, which we already suspected. Moreover, the father does not undervalue women, and has not attempted to suppress his dominating wife.

> "The physical history of the boy is as follows: the mother was in labor twelve hours at his birth, but no instruments were used. There was some difficulty in the labor and during his birth the boy's face became quite blue. He weighed twelve pounds at birth."

This point of the difficult delivery is not as important as may be believed. Probably the child had a large head. It is quite common for boys to have larger heads than girls when they are born.

> "Mother says he was not a pretty baby and had a yellow skin when he was born. At two months he broke out in a rash which remained until he was fifteen months old. He held up his head at an early age and sat up at six months. First tooth appeared at eight months, and at this time he was weaned. There was considerable trouble with feeding, and until a proper formula was found, his bowels were inflamed. At the age of nine months he began to eat solid food. At fifteen months the mother began to train him to keep dry, and at two years he had full control of his bladder. He was given a little cod-liver oil as a child. The mother noticed something was wrong when he got bigger and bigger but did not speak. He walked at two years."

Only the physician who was present at birth can give us the proper information about the yellow skin and the early rash. It is presumable that he had rickets as a child if he did not learn to walk until he was two years old.

> "He communicated by motions and a few sounds which the family understood and the mother understood best."

It is very unfortunate that the mother understood these motions of the child. As talking was unnecessary it is not surprising that he had little desire to develop speech.

> "There is no hearing defect. The doctor told the mother not to worry about the boy but to leave him alone because some day 'things would dawn on him.' The boy began to talk at the age of five. His adenoids and tonsils have been removed. He has never been sick and he eats everything."

It is not uncommon for children whose whims have all been gratified, not to talk until after the fourth year. On the other hand, it is usual to hear that these children have many food fads or that they wet the bed. As our patient does not do these things, we may conclude that he has maintained such a favorable situation with his mother that he feels no need to improve it.

> "For the past two years he has been wearing glasses to correct a defective vision (20/70). He learned to dress himself about a year and a half ago. He has to be constantly urged to dress himself, as he dawdles a long time, and it takes him considerable time to determine which shoe goes on which foot. He is bigger and heavier than most children of his age (five feet tall, weighs one hundred pounds)."

That he did not learn to dress himself until he was ten years old is a certain sign that he has been badly spoiled. He is not very much interested in dressing himself, because he wants his mother to help him. The fact that he is larger than children of his age may be a symptom of a diseased pituitary gland, but on the other hand it may simply be a sign that he is a healthy child and that his mother has fed him well.

> "He writes with his right hand but does everything else with his left hand."

This is a very important point because it assures us that he is congenitally a left-handed child who has been confronted and discouraged by the problems of adjusting himself to a right-handed world.

> "The boy has always been closer to his mother and older sister. He seldom mentions his father."

It is a common situation among pampered children who spend the greatest part of their time with their mother, that the father cannot compete with the mother. This father has really made a great mistake, especially by being hopeless about the boy. I am sure that the older sister could win our patient over, but his reconciliation with the father is a more difficult problem. As long as the mother is present the child will always turn toward her. The father should take the boy away on a trip, show him a good time and become his "pal." At some time he should confess to Robert that his opinion of his intelligence was mistaken. Our treatment should begin with the reconciliation of the boy and his father.

"The mother sends him on errands, and he likes to go and talks about it. If she wants two or more items from the store she must write them on a slip of paper. Since this report was begun, the storekeeper suggested that the mother give him no slip, and an improvement has been noticed."

We can hardly expect a child who is not accustomed to function alone to remember two or more items when he is sent to the store. The storekeeper, however, understands the boy and has good insight into his situation. There are many laymen who have such understanding. The fact that an improvement has been noticed, indeed, that there are possibilities of improvement, is a very good sign. It leads us to believe that most of the bad mistakes that we find can be obviated.

"Sometimes the mother notices him talking to a make-believe child, and answering for him. It is usually a boy with whom he is speaking. Then he talks rough and ready, like a street boy. His face becomes animated and he seems to be fighting."

Many children play this game of talking to a fictitious child, and it is very interesting that this boy who could not talk for such a long time now trains himself to speak, not only for himself, but also for another child. Robert might even develop into a writer or a dramatist. Left-handed children are often inclined to be artistic. We may also infer from his game and the fact that he quarrels with his sisters, that he longs for the companionship of a boy. He has probably already developed a certain fear of women and an overvaluation of their power, especially if his mother is a dominating woman. He evidently has a lively imagination —which is very common in timid children. It is easy to be heroic, gallant, and courageous, in a day-dream. Really, he is a coward, and yet it hurts him to believe this and so in his imagination he makes believe that he is a conqueror. What we have to do is to show him the way to be courageous in reality.

> "He does not play with the boys in the street. He says, 'The boys in the street will not play my way; they are always fighting and I don't like to fight.' Sometimes he has quiet laughing spells, which the mother fears. These are greater at times, and then almost disappear."

He does not play with the boys in the street because he is timid, while the laughing spells that the mother fears are instruments with which he can weaken her domination. Probably they are most violent when she does not give way to him, or indulge him sufficiently.

> "Sometimes in sleep he sits up in bed, talks to himself about various things, then quietly lies down and sleeps without anyone interfering."

Many children scream at night in order to bring their mothers to them. This boy is satisfied merely to give his mother a hint.

> "In school he tries to make friends but is easily discouraged. The children do not avoid him or call him names. Although he has had many teachers he can recall but two of the names of preceding ones."

If a pampered child does not make friends easily, he soon gives up trying. So far as his memory is concerned, he does not remember the names of his teachers because he did not like them. This is not so much a lack of memory, as it is a desire to forget.

> "It is only recently that he began to speak to the children around him in school. He entered school at the age of six, spent two terms in 1A, three in 1B, two in 2A, two in 2B, one in 3A, two in 3B, now being in 3B for the second time."

The fact that he does not speak to other children shows again how isolated our patient is. Nevertheless, he is beginning to improve. It is fortunate that he began school at the age of six, and not at a later age. His constant repetition of classes is hardly calculated to encourage him, and we can understand that he is not very much interested in school. It will be our duty to give him hope. One way to do this is to give him some good reports in school, even though his work is not excellent. This policy is not as erroneous as it sounds. There is little sense in discouraging this boy by giving him bad reports, and my recommendation is not to give him any reports until he has made some progress. It might be well to give him easier tasks in school, which the teacher is convinced he can accomplish. She should find out his special interests, and encourage him to work along those lines. It is the teacher's task to show him that he can really be a worth-while pupil. I know that it is very difficult to do this in public schools, and I know the objection may be raised that the other children will believe Robert is preferred to them. My answer to this is, that a feeling must be developed which will enable the entire class to help the teacher deal with the child. It will help our patient if the other pupils cooperate in helping him.

> "His handwriting is that of the 7th grade child."

Here is one field in which he is advanced. He has trained his hands. This is a compensation for his deficiency as a left-handed child. Nevertheless, the boy is discouraged in spite of conquering this particular handicap. Many individuals prefer to be influenced by their defeats rather than by their successes, and in the pattern of a timid child defeat is often valued more highly than success.

> "His drawing is poor."

In spite of this statement, I believe that Robert could develop considerable facility in drawing or designing if his interest were aroused. This would be one of the compensations for his poor eyes. The teacher says that he wears glasses in school, but perhaps he has not trained his eyes because he does not like to wear them.

"He is very backward in reading."

It is well known that some left-handed children are slow in reading because they tend to reverse the letters in the word. Perhaps Robert belongs to this type of left-handed individual. One of my students, Dr. Alice Friedman, made the discovery that left-handed children reverse and twist the letters in words when they read. Movements from left to right are normal for right-handed people, whereas left-handed people move more easily from right to left, and this fundamental tendency permeates the entire psyche. A left-handed child whose peculiarity is not recognized, experiences a number of failures in school, and eventually is no longer interested, because he cannot compete in reading with right-handed children. It is no wonder that his progress stops, for his misfortunes in reading and drawing are projected toward all the problems he must face. If we find that Robert is suffering from the reading disability associated with left-handedness, we must try to correct his training.

There are a number of signs which will help us. If he twists the letters of a word in spelling, or if you ask him to draw an animal and he draws it moving from right to left, or places his left thumb on top when he clasps his hand, it is presumptive evidence that he is left-handed.

> "In spelling he has three tricks. He knows the word; he knows the word and inverts two letters, or he doesn't know the word and almost invariably begins it with 'e.' The teacher attributes the last two to his left-handedness."

I believe this is only a symptom of his despair, he does not know how to go on.*

> "In March, 1926, he was examined by the inspector of the ungraded classes. He was then eight years old and he attained a mental age of four years, six months."

We can easily see how the suspicion might grow that this boy is feeble-minded, but intelligence tests are not definitive, and must not stop our diagnosis. We know that an over-petted child is so frightened by his defeats in school that he does not concentrate in taking the test and the results are not reliable. The low intelligence quotient fits into the pattern of a spoiled child just as well as it does into that of a feeble-minded child. The psychological tests are valuable only when

* Editor's note: As a great many words end in "e," and the natural tendency of this child is to begin a word from the end, it is reasonable to suspect that this is an important sign of his left-handedness.

they coincide with all our other findings, but in this case the boy's failures are due to his wish to be supported by his mother and to his deep discouragement.

> "His intelligence quotient according to the Stanford-Binet Test, was 52, the basal year was 3, the upper limits 7. The achievement in reading according to the Haggerty Reading Test, is that of a 1A child. The achievement in arithmetic according to the Woody-McCall Mixed Fundamental Test is that of a 1A child. The boy is very attractive and pleasant and cooperates well in the test."

The last sentence gives us another reason for his being spoiled and shows also that he is intelligent enough to make capital of his attractiveness.

> "His reaction time is quick, and his attention good. He habitually repeated the last word he had spoken, but the present teacher does not find that he does this."

The repetition of words is a sign of uncertainty and an attempt to win time by hesitating and stammering. Very likely his present teacher does not find this fault because she does not press him so much and he is not afraid of her.

> "The boy is seriously retarded in mental development and fails to distinguish colors and forms. (He had no glasses at this time.)"

There is no doubt that there is an organic inferiority of the eye, and he may be color-blind as well. The fact that he cannot distinguish forms indicates a lack of proper training.

> "His memory for digits is equal to a four-year child, while his memory for thoughts is equal to a three-year child."

This information seems really discouraging, but we know that intelligent adult persons under severe strain may be unable to count, and Robert's emotions and attitudes, during the examination, are important factors in deciding its importance.

> "He was recommended for the ungraded classes, but as his mother would not consent, he was put with the other children in the slow-progress class. He claims he has no dreams."

If he has no dreams it is a sign that he is entirely satisfied with his present situation, that he has arrived at his goal of being thoroughly indulged and that the world presents no problems to him. He has attained security at home and at school, and he does not strive any more.

> "At first he claims that he has no childhood remembrances, but states, 'A little girl used to let me ride on her bicycle.' This happened recently, but he speaks of it as if it had happened a long time ago."

This remembrance fits into his pattern: he wants everyone to be his servant.

> "Ambition: at one time he wanted to be big enough to do his own spelling; at another time he wanted to sweep the store for his father."

If he expressed the first ambition independently, it is a good indication that he understands his deficiencies and expects to overcome them in the future, while the second ambition shows that he wants to be liked by his father also.

> "Another ambition is to be big enough to play around in the street; he does not want to work to earn money. Given three wishes, he chooses: to be big, to be strong, to learn his lessons. The first two came quite spontaneously."

We find a note of discouragement again in his desire to avoid work. So far as his ambitions are concerned, I believe the first two are the wish of every boy, especially in America where athletics play such an important rôle. That he wants to learn his lessons, shows where the trouble lies.

> "Given his choice of staying in the house to read a book or going on the street, he chooses the second. The teacher believes this is a case of a discouraged youngest child handicapped by the clumsiness of his large size and his left-handedness. The parents have been told to give him re-

sponsibilities, to notice his useful activities, and to avoid praising his sisters in his presence. The teacher has given him responsibility in the classroom, such as distributing paper and ventilating the room. He is quick to watch for the signal. At first he showed little judgment in the amount of paper he took, but an improvement has been noticed."

The teacher has chosen the very best way to help this child, and I could not recommend any better. I should like to explain to this child that some mistakes in his education have been made. I want to encourage him to believe that he can rise to his sisters' level, and explain to him that he has not succeeded because he has been too dependent on his mother and lost confidence in himself. We must assure him of his success even if it does not come immediately. We can use the analogy of learning to swim, where all initial movements are wrong—or otherwise one could swim from the very beginning. You cannot swim right away, but you can learn it in the end. We must put the proposition to the boy in terms that he can understand.

The child must also understand that he has to make better contacts with his playmates. I should place him in a group or a club after school hours, so that he would be more with strangers and less with his mother. We must explain the specific difficulties that he has in reading and reeducate him to read correctly. If we can lift him from his hopelessness he will improve. The last points of the case history show that he is already on the right path, and I am sure that the teacher will notice an improvement. Furthermore, we must speak with the mother and explain to her that he is an intelligent child, but that she will be able to enjoy his intelligence only if she makes him independent. It is clear from the difficulties of this case why spoiled children contribute the largest percentage of problem children.

## Conference

The mother enters.

Dr. Adler. We should like to talk to you about Robert. We believe that he is an intelligent boy, and that his difficulties are largely due to the fact that he does not see any necessity for acting independently so long as you solve his problems for him. It is possible for you to correct the situation. You must make him more independent, put him among strange children, and let him live more among his playmates. Let him join a club or a play group in his free time. It is not good for Robert to be with you so much, because he knows how to influence you and always knows what to expect from you. We also believe that the child is left-handed and that this left-handedness is the cause of much of his trouble, especially in reading and spelling. If he is correctly taught he can learn to read and spell as well as any other child, but at present he is discouraged, and refuses to go on because he has failed so often. You must let him wash and dress himself, and do not nag him if he makes a mistake. It would also be well to have this boy more closely connected with his father. You should tell your husband to give Robert a chance. It would be well for the father to take him away for a few days on a trip and make a comrade of him. The boy must be told in so many words that his father believes in his success. It is my opinion that he is a normal child, and if you will give me permission, I shall talk to him now to see whether I can influence him to be more independent.

MOTHER. I know he will be very much frightened. I am frightened myself because I did not expect to see such an audience.

The boy is called for. As he enters the room the mother says, "Come on, Buster," and he goes straight to his mother and puts his arms around her.

DR. ADLER. Must you protect your mother? I do not think she will fall. I think she can stand up by herself. Would you like to be supported by your mother all the time or be a grown-up man?

ROBERT. A grown-up man.

DR. ADLER. Would you rather work alone or would you rather have others work for you?

ROBERT. I should like to have my mother work for me.

DR. ADLER. It is very nice to like your mother, but you cannot expect her to do everything for you. You would be happier if you did more things for yourself. You must begin to do things alone. Other children begin very early, and you have had some trouble because you have begun late. But you can help yourself if you begin right away to do everything alone: brush your teeth, wash yourself, and dress yourself alone. Do not let your mother interfere with you. Wouldn't it be much nicer if you could do things by yourself? Have you learned to swim?

ROBERT. Yes.

DR. ADLER. Don't you remember that it was hard work at first? I am sure it took you some time to learn to swim as well as you do now. Whatever you do is hard in the beginning, but after a while you succeed. If you can learn to swim, you can also learn to read and do your arithmetic, but you must keep at it, have patience, and not always expect your mother to do it for you. I am sure that you can do it. Do not worry because others can do better than you. Your teacher tells me that you have made some improvement recently. That is splendid. How would you like to have some friends to play with? How would you like to join a club?

ROBERT. It would be very nice.

DR. ADLER. We will find you a jolly club, where you can play and talk and show how independent you are. I think it would be nice if you were to take a trip with your father, too.

Robert leaves the room with his mother.

Discussion by the class:

STUDENT. Should we teach a left-handed person to write with the right hand?

DR. ADLER. I think this is a good thing to do for two reasons. In the first place, our entire civilization is right-handed. In the second place, if a person always uses the left hand, he is conspicuous. He is apt to believe that he is different or unequal. You have no doubt seen rather uncomplimentary statistics about left-handed people, but my statistics show that many of them are artistic, especially when they have trained the weak right hand. There is a superstition that if you train a left-handed child to use the right hand he will become a stutterer. We should not take this superstition seriously. To be sure, when the training is done in a mistaken way, and the child is reproached and humiliated, he may show his maladjustment by stuttering. I consider it very important that a teacher know whether a child is essentially left-handed or right-handed, because if a left-handed child is laboring under difficulties we know that mistakes are being made about him whose effects may last for years.

STUDENT. What would you do in a case where a ten-year-old boy, ready for junior high, uses both hands and is very precocious? Attempting to write with his right hand makes him nervous; he cries, and says he won't do it.

DR. ADLER. That is because he has been badly trained.

STUDENT. He plays the piano very well.

DR. ADLER. You could use his interest in the piano in training the right hand. This should be done by someone not personally interested, who can speak to the child only from a scientific point of view. You see, by playing the piano, he can exercise both hands.

STUDENT. Would you suggest manual training for a left-handed child?

DR. ADLER. Yes, by all means. You know that many left-handed ball-players and prize-fighters train themselves so that they are much quicker with the right hand than with the left. Success always comes to those who struggle for it, and this is especially true of left-handed people in the arts. But let us get back to our case. We see that Robert's greatest problem is his school work. Do you remember how he came into the room and immediately clung to his mother? This is characteristic of his whole life; he wants his mother to support him. You will see how he will improve in a short while if he carries out our instructions.

STUDENT. Would you advise corporal punishment for such a child, under any circumstances?

DR. ADLER. You ought to be convinced that I am entirely against all corporal punishment. The method I use is to learn the circumstances of early childhood, to explain and to persuade. What possible result could you gain by beating such a child? We have no justification for beating a child because he is a school failure. He is not able to read, because he has not been properly trained, and spanking would not improve the training. The only result would be that the child would reconcile himself to being spanked for his failures, and would become a truant in order to escape an unpleasant situation. Look at the spanking from the child's point of view and you will see that it only increases the difficulty. In passing, let me say that only those people beat children who do not understand what else to do with them.

EDITOR'S NOTE. After the conference in Dr. Adler's class this patient was seen by the editor and was treated for a period of months. A thorough examination showed that the child was suffering from an aggravated form of dyslexia strephosymbolica, the specific reading disability of left-handed children. His left-handedness was very marked and was indicated, not only by a complete preponderance of the left half of his body, but also by his preference for left-handed actions in all intuitive and early formed motor reactions. The child had no conception of the inner structure of words, twisted the letters within the words, confused the plus and the multiplication signs, and had practically no idea of the correlation of the sounds of individual letters in the alphabet. He was taught to read by a kinesthetic method devised by the editor, so that at the end of two months' treatment he was able to read books far in advance of his school age. It was with great difficulty that the mother was persuaded to allow the child to come alone to the consultations and she never consented to his going to a boy's camp. Although great progress has been made in this case, it is probable that the boy will always be inhibited and will never attain a complete independence, not because of any inherent defect, but because of the emotional fixations of his mother.

## *THE ROAD TO CRIME*

THE case we have tonight is that of an eight-year-old boy. The first notes of the case history are the following:

> "Carl T., age eight years, two months, class 2B, I.Q. 98, whose present problem is that he lies to his family, teacher, and other boys. He has committed some thefts, and has been lying and stealing since the age of five. Before this time there was no problem."

As Carl's average intelligent quotient is 98, we may safely conclude that he is not a feeble-minded child. Lying is a sign of the child's insecurity and weakness. When we hear of a child who lies, it is wise to learn in the very beginning whether he tells boastful lies or whether there is someone in the environment of whom he is afraid. Perhaps the child wishes to avoid punishment, scolding, and humiliation.

It is stated in the case history that he has lied and stolen since the age of five, but before that was not a problem child. If this observation is correct we may assume that a crisis in the boy's life occurred in his fifth year. It is probable that he has an inferiority complex, and is more interested in himself than in anyone else. He steals, which signifies that he feels humiliated and tries to increase his self-esteem in a useless way.

> "The mother told the teacher in confidence that she was never married to the child's father. Her mother died when she was very young and at the age of sixteen she was seduced by a friend of her father whom she never saw subsequently, and who never knew that she gave birth to a child."

It is usually very difficult to develop social interest in an illegitimate child. In our prevailing civilization illegitimacy is considered a disgrace, and a child with this background is put on the defensive. Carl has been brought up in a difficult situation. A large percentage of illegitimate children develop into criminals, drunkards, sexual perverts, and so on, because they have been badly handicapped and are attracted by illicit modes of behavior which seem to promise a short cut to happiness. In this case the father has been absent, and the boy has lacked still another normal opportunity for developing social feeling.

> "When he was five years old his mother married. The stepfather has a child of his own, a girl two years older than Carl."

Carl's trouble began in his fifth year, when his mother married. Probably he felt that the one person with whom he had made an adequate social contact was taken away from him by his mother's husband. We may presume that he came to the conclusion, "Nobody is interested in me." The introduction of a sister into the family offered an additional complicating factor, because his mother probably had to take care of this child too. Perhaps this girl was well developed, beloved by her father, and a well-behaved child, making the difficulty even greater for Carl. He was only five years old, after all, and his former experience had not been of a kind to develop sufficient courage and strength to face this new situation. So he became a problem child.

> "There are now two other children, a sister two and one-half and a brother one and one-half years old."

These two other children narrow his position still further. In all probability, his pattern has been built up in such a way that he actually believes the others are preferred by his parents.

> "Until he was two years old he lived with his mother. Then the mother went to work in a children's nursery, and for three months he was on a nursery farm in Connecticut. He was unhappy at the farm and came home so frightened that he ran away from everyone."

During the two years that he was with his mother, Carl was probably interested only in her. Evidently his experiences at the farm were not conducive to a development of his slight social feeling.

> "He stayed with his mother six months, until she went to work for a doctor whose children she cared for. Carl was boarded in a near-by home, and his mother saw him daily. He was very happy there and remained in the home until his mother married when he was five years old. Both parents are members of the Salvation Army and the father plays in the Salvation Army band."

Carl was happy only when he was close to his mother. The occupation of the parents is evidence that they probably are quite poor.

> "The mother cried the first time she was interviewed by the teacher, and said, 'I do not know what to do about Carl.' "

We know that it is very bad for a child if his parents are discouraged about him. The child is justified then in losing all hope himself, and when a child is hopeless the last vestiges of his social interest are lost.

> "The father beats him with a razor strop when he is bad. He goes to Sunday school regularly and last week attended a new Sunday school. He was given fifteen cents, ten cents for car-fare and five cents for the collection. After he had gone, his mother wondered whether he had taken the right street-car and went to the corner to look for him.

> She saw him coming from a candy store where he had spent ten cents for candy."

These are important facts, because we have found the severe person whom we presupposed in the environment. The candy store is a simple compensation for a child who feels himself discriminated against. Such a child has not many ways to compensate, and the candy store is one of the most common.

> "He came to school lately, bringing the teacher a box of candy."

From the fact that he tries to bribe his teacher to like him, we may conclude that he was once a spoiled child and remembers the pleasures of being indulged.

> "He had four and a half dollars which he said belonged to his mother. It was the change he had obtained from the candy store. The teacher put the money in an envelope and kept it for him until dismissal time. Then she returned it to him, impressing him with the fact that he must return the money to his mother. When Carl returned to school at one o'clock and was asked whether he had returned the money, he answered, 'Yes.' "

No child in such a situation would answer in the negative. We cannot expect a child to admit stealing.

"A short time later the teacher noticed that many of his classmates had new toys and some of them money they had received from Carl."

He wants to bribe his playmates as well as his teacher, and we must conclude that he feels a lack of affection and appreciation. It is not surprising that he behaves badly, that he is a problem boy, and that he is treated as an outcast, but we must realize that to Carl all this is a confirmation of the central thesis of his life. "The others are preferred."

"The teacher said that his mother was sent for, and after many lies as to where he got the money, he finally confessed that he took it from an aunt who was visiting them."

In cases of this kind the teacher must be very tactful in her investigation. It was wise to speak with the mother first and not allow the other children to know of his theft.

"Carl was a normal, healthy child until he was two years old, but since then has been rather weak. He asks to leave the room many times a day. The mother has had him examined by a physician, but no kidney trouble is present. He masturbates frequently in school."

These facts further indicate that Carl wishes to gain the attention of his teacher in the schoolroom. When he cannot do it by bribing his teachers and classmates, he does it by masturbating.

"He wets the bed every night of his life."

If this is true, we can be certain that the mother has not fulfilled her functions correctly in teaching him how to be clean.

> "He was deprived of dessert, but it had no effect on his bed-wetting. He went without dessert for six months. He was promised twenty-five cents if he would stop for a week, but he did not stop even for a single night."

If his pattern demands attention from his mother, none of these methods will cause him to relinquish so important a weapon against her as bed-wetting. How could this boy stop? His goal is a goal of useless superiority: to be the center of attention. He must follow this pattern, and if he is stopped in one way he will increase his efforts to gain attention another way. Depriving such a child of dessert will only increase his desire for candy. His mother's method of compelling him to stop his bed-wetting deepened Carl's feeling of degradation. He has lost hope of ever winning proper appreciation from his family, but he still knows how to be the center of attention.

> "He has had the mumps and a severe case of whooping cough. Two years ago he had stomach

trouble and was on a strict diet for a year, but since this time has had no further trouble."

It is unusual for a child to have stomach trouble which demands a strict diet for an entire year, and the diet complicated by the deprivation of desserts gives us an interesting picture of his environment.

"His earliest recollection is that at the age of two he threw his mother's dresser-set out of the window and boys from the street brought it back to the house. 'I didn't get punished because I was too young.' "

It is not unusual to find mismanaged children throwing things out of the window when they feel they are not being sufficiently indulged. I know of another case in which a child, who had a sister some years younger than he, threw everything he could lay his hands on, out of the window; he was punished for his misbehavior until he developed an anxiety neurosis. This anxiety neurosis was centered about the fear that he might throw something out of the window, and so the boy cried all day. He had found another way to gain attention in his exaggerated terror that he would be naughty again.

When you punish a child of this type you only aggravate his condition, for he has no real understanding of the circumstances. Should you ask the child whether he is neglected or discriminated against in his family, he will usually answer, "No," but you will see that he is always doing things whose meaning seems to be, "Watch me more closely." Lying, masturbation, stealing, and wetting the bed are all instruments which the child unconsciously uses because he wants to be observed and is afraid that he will be overlooked.

It is interesting to note that Carl's earliest recollection is connected with the idea of punishment. He seems to say that there was a time when he could have avoided punishment, but that he would be punished if he did these things today. We know that there are children who really do not object to being beaten. When you beat them, they simply say to themselves, "I must be more cunning and not be discovered." This is excellent training for a career of crime, which is precisely what we are afraid of in this case.

> "It is his ambition to be a doctor. His oldest sister is going to be a nurse, and he wants to be in the same hospital."

His real ambition is to be ahead of everyone else with the least effort, and his desire to be a doctor is his method of making his ambition concrete. As he has been sick and has suffered a great deal and his mother has been working in a hospital, we can imagine that to be a doctor is Carl's equivalent to being very close to God. Moreover, he wants to be at least the equal of his oldest sister and he knows already that a doctor in the hospital holds a higher position than a nurse. It is the typical striving of the second child to surpass the older child. It is a simple and common story, but Carl's preparation has been especially bad. Obviously the boy is on the defensive, and our treatment must be directed toward making him feel that he is the equal of his brother and sisters and not undervalued by his family. We can do this by explaining that he can win more significance by good behavior than by bad.

The father must be taught to conciliate the child, rather than to punish him with a razor strap. I am sure that this father who works in the Salvation Army would listen to such advice, and I believe that the mother too could be influenced in the right direction. To be sure, the difficulties are very great, and if it proves impossible to make Carl's home happier for him than it now is, with a despairing mother and a stern father and with his brother and sisters preferred to him, it may be necessary to remove the boy to a more favorable environment.

We must explain to the mother the circumstances that make it possible for Carl to feel he is neglected. Children often make mistakes because they do not understand their situation. The mother is the important member of the family to influence, because it will be easier for her to make him feel appreciated. Carl must be instructed to make friends and we might suggest that it is not necessary to bribe people if he is interested in them, and faithful to them. This case gives a very good idea of the origin of criminality in the family situation. It is entirely useless to wait until a boy has committed a hold-up, before we consider him a criminal. This is the point at which we should start.

## Conference

STUDENT. Do you believe the religious training and exercises of the father have influenced this child to go in an opposite direction? The Salvation Army people are very strict and make their children do penance every night for the wrongs they have committed during the day.

DR. ADLER. I doubt whether there are any further reasons for this boy's behavior than those I have described. You must be careful not to read ideas into a case history which are not actually there. If I had heard that he suffers under the pressure of some authoritative religious idea, I might consider your point, but no such pressure was mentioned. Nevertheless your interpretation may be valuable, but from a different angle. If this boy became thoroughly rebellious he might attack his parents at the point where they are most sensitive: in other words, he might attack their religion. Recently some interesting statistics were published by a very good German sociologist, who found that a striking proportion of criminals came from the families of people who were occupied with the enforcement of the law. No one has been able to explain why the children of judges, lawyers, and teachers are so often criminals. It seems to me that the only explanation lies in the point I have just mentioned—that belligerent children attack their parents at the point of greatest sensitivity. Perhaps that is why we find so many illnesses in the families of doctors.

The mother of Carl is sent for but she is reluctant to enter the room.

Dr. Adler. The hesitant attitude of this mother indicates her lack of courage. Perhaps she is also ashamed to speak openly about her boy's misdeeds. Perhaps she does not come because she is crying. We will do what we can to console her and encourage her. Some of you may wonder why I don't go out to her. I know that she expects me to, but I shall wait here, because I rather imagine she believes we are very much excited about the case of her son. I want to talk to her quietly about his misbehavior, as though it were quite usual and easily corrected.

The mother enters the room.

Dr. Adler. I find that Carl's faults are not extraordinary, although I know that many families and teachers consider them tragedies. Children cannot always develop in the correct way. I once went into a classroom and asked, "Who in this room has never stolen anything?" and I found that every child had stolen something. The teacher too admitted that he had stolen things. Therefore we need not look upon stealing as very terrible, especially, as a child gets much discouraged if he feels that his mother is hopeless about him. It would be better if you tried to win Carl's confidence, and encouraged him to believe that you are quite hopeful about his future. How does he act toward the other children in the family?

MOTHER. He seems to be very fond of them.

DR. ADLER. Is he sometimes jealous?

MOTHER. He has a stepsister, and I think there is a little jealousy between them.

DR. ADLER. Is the stepsister well developed, very bright, and much beloved?

MOTHER. Yes.

DR. ADLER. I have often found that if one child in the family is making great progress, the other children are afraid to compete. It is hard to avoid this situation, and I think therefore it would be well if you could reconcile these two children. I believe that your son thinks he is not liked. He lies and commits other misdeeds because he is in an unhappy situation. Give him the impression that he will be pardoned and that you understand why he felt jealous and inferior. With encouragement, he will become a better pupil in school, and a good child all around if he can be reconciled with his stepsister. Does the child depend upon you a great deal?

MOTHER. Yes.

DR. ADLER. Does he depend as much upon his father?

MOTHER. He thinks a lot of his father, but does not seem so close to him.

Dr. Adler. Do you believe that it would be possible to see that his father gives Carl a chance? Have them take occasional walks together and talk about nature and the world. Has the father time for this?

Mother. Yes, I think he would do it.

Dr. Adler. After a great deal of experience with this kind of boy, it is my belief that his behavior will be greatly improved as soon as he feels he is loved as much as the other children. His present conduct shows that he lacks confidence in his ability to develop as well as his stepsister, but this mistake in his thinking can be corrected by showing him how to win your approval. Then if he did make a mistake, I would not punish him as you have heretofore. I think you must be convinced, by now, that there is no advantage in spanking him or in depriving him of his dessert. If he should lie or steal again, say to him, "Do you feel that you are being treated unfairly again? Tell me what you want." Such a conversation would make a great impression upon Carl. I also believe that in this same way you could help him to remain clean at night. It has been my experience that children wet the bed because they want someone to take care of them. You see, if you have to get up at night to attend to his wants, he feels that you are taking care of him as you did when he was a baby. Is he afraid of the dark?

Mother. Nothing seems to affect him very much.

Dr. Adler. We are probably correct in thinking that his misdeeds are committed because he has lost all hope of competing with his sister for his parents' affection. Would you like to have me try to encourage Carl?

MOTHER. Yes.

The mother goes out of the room.

DR. ADLER. You see we have found the correct clue: jealousy toward the stepsister. I think we can relieve him from this unpleasant situation.

The boy comes in.

DR. ADLER. I understand that you are a good pupil in school. If you are attentive and work hard, your friends and your teacher will like you. If you do work hard, I am sure that you will be as good in school as your sister is. Would you like that?

CARL. Yes.

DR. ADLER. They tell me that you want to be a doctor. It is a very nice profession. I also am a doctor. To be a good doctor, you must be more interested in others than yourself, so that you can understand what they need when they are sick. You must try to be a good friend and not think too much about yourself. It is not really friendship if I give somebody a present so that he will be nice to me, but if I like him and do not lie to him he will be a real friend. I am sure that you can do this. And I am going to ask you sometime whether you have. I know that your sister is older than you are and therefore knows a little more than you do, but that does not matter. If you behaved in such a way that you were not scolded or punished, you would soon catch up with her and be as well liked as she is. Would that please you?

CARL. Yes.

DR. ADLER. You must also be a good friend to your sister and be interested in her. Does she like you?

CARL. Yes.

DR. ADLER. Then it is very easy. All you have to do is not to disturb her when she works and help her when you can. See whether you can find out how she works, and then do the same thing, so that you can be on equal terms with her. You really cannot make yourself any better by taking things from her or from your mother. You must wait and do your work and show how valuable you are. Sometimes we are treated unjustly, but we must be strong enough not to be unfair ourselves. To be interested in others and not cheat them, is a good way to win people's love.

Boy leaves the room.

DR. ADLER. I have spoken to this boy as I have, because I am certain that he does not realize why he lies and steals. He's utterly discouraged, and in his perplexity is striving frantically to make his position secure. The parents should now guarantee this boy his natural measure of love and affection.

TEACHER. The father says that he prefers his daughter.

DR. ADLER. We will have to instruct the father not to show his preference, and to this end I propose the simple expedient of having him take a walk with the boy and talk with him, so that Carl will feel honored and appreciated and somehow sense the fact that his father is interested in him.

STUDENT. What should the mother do if he lies and steals again?

DR. ADLER. The mother should say to him, "Have you lost hope of competing with your sister again? I am sure that you can succeed, but not by lying and stealing." Above all, the mother should not despair. Not infrequently children of this kind commit suicide later in life, and we must try to avoid such an outcome.

## *THE BOY WHO WANTS TO LEAD*

THIS evening we are to consider the case of John, who is almost nine years old. This is his present problem:

> "Difficulties with other children. He loves to fight at all times. In school he disturbs his class and attempts to be noticed by acting silly. He has no social adjustment with other children and wants constantly to be in the limelight."

If a boy has difficulties with other children, it is probable that he lacks social interest, and if he fights to gain attention we may presume that he is not brave enough to face the problems of life in a useful way.

> "The parents have always had as great trouble with him at home as his teacher has at school. He has been very mischievous and does not obey orders."

As John's behavior at home and at school is identical, he evidently considers the two situations to be similar. We may conclude therefore that he is properly appreciated neither in the home nor at school. That he is very mischievous and does not obey orders promptly, is not astonishing, because we cannot expect a rebel to be obedient—that would be a contradiction.

> "The mother says that he had a very strict nurse for sixteen months when he was a young baby. No one, not even his father, was allowed to enter his room after six at night."

Apparently the nurse was strict with the parents too, and while I think that it is wise for a child not to be disturbed when he is asleep, I do not understand why he should not be seen if he is awake. The boy was evidently connected only with this one nurse, and as she lacked the skill to develop his social interest, he grew up under a certain disadvantage. The point will be tested later when we learn his earliest recollection.

> "The family constellation consists of a father, a mother, the patient, and a younger sister almost three years old."

This is a very familiar constellation. The boy is nearly nine and there was a long period during which he was the only child. It is improbable that his rebellious attitude can be traced to the birth of the younger sister; it is more probable that he has developed the characteristics of an only child. It is a little hard to understand why he needs to fight for sufficient attention. Perhaps something has happened in his life which has aggravated the situation.

"The relationship of the parents is normal and happy. The father is the only one the boy obeys. Formerly he was extremely strict with him and punished him severely when he did wrong."

We know that if a marriage is unhappy it hinders the development of the child's social theory. On the other hand, the child of very congenial parents may be kept too long in the position of a baby and acquire a dangerous feeling of inferiority to them. Parents should not show too much affection for each other in the presence of the child. If John obeys only his father, then it is probable that the mother is weak and the child chooses her to attack. Punishment is the best way I know to stunt the social feeling. It is possible that John developed some sort of social feeling toward his nurse and his mother, but cannot establish any bond with his father, who has inflicted corporal punishment. The child may actually begin to hate his father and wish he would go away or die. Such an attitude is always the result of maladjustment—the Freudian Œdipus complex. It is an artificial problem. You can develop the Œdipus complex in a child by beating him, as you can prevent it by developing the child's social interest toward each parent.

"He is mischievous and troublesome when left alone with his mother. She is very nervous, and he makes her unhappy because he will not obey her. He knows he can easily have his own way

> with her. She can do nothing with him. Therefore, the father takes entire charge of the training and discipline of the boy."

John's mother is unwise in complaining about her pains and aches before the child. The child is always the stronger, and there is no use fighting stronger people. We do not know what she means when she says that "he will not obey her." Perhaps she demands too much of him. It is never desirable that a child should obey like a dog. There should be a comradely relationship between parents and children. I have seen too many parents who insisted on blind, unreasoning obedience. This mother's behavior is that of a hopeless person who has declared her intellectual bankruptcy to the child and turned the whole matter over to his father.

> "The little girl is very smart, obedient, and lovable. The parents often remind John how careful and obedient his little sister is, and her conduct is given as a pattern to follow."

Very often, if one child in the family is disobedient, the conduct of the other child is held up as an example. The obedient child is not necessarily kind and good by nature, but may be merely an opportunist who has learned the advantages of propitiation. I remember the instance of a family in which one daughter became violently rebellious when a younger girl was born. This younger child was always very sweet, was much praised by the parents and became a model child because she found it the best way to get everything she wanted. Yet, when this younger child went to school, overindulgence ceased, and she spent the rest of her life debating every problem because she did not have the courage to risk making a mistake. She had no friends, no occupation, and she could never fall in love and was never married. Because she could find no useful channel for her desire to be a model person and the center of attention, she began to suffer from a compulsion neurosis, which expressed itself in unremitting efforts to keep everything spotlessly clean. By the feeling that she was the purest and cleanest person in the world she obtained her goal of superiority, and she believed herself defiled by everyone who approached or touched her. In John's case, the younger sister probably enjoys being a pattern, perhaps not so much from social interest as from a feeling of pride and an ambition to be the adored favorite. Nevertheless, we need not be surprised to hear that this boy likes his sister. Nor should we be astonished to hear the opposite. Both situations may exist in a case like this.

> "John does not seem to resent the parents' praises of the younger sister. He says she is cute and that he loves her very much. The mother is afraid that he will teach her bad tricks and that it will spoil her sweet manner. She has already been seen making faces and imitating him."

Probably John does not resent his sister's sweetness, because he thinks his fighting attitude is the superior technique. He finds that he can gain more power in that way than by obedience, and it seems as if the little sister were beginning to agree with him.

> "The mother and father have a fine store which they operate together. The mother leaves at nine in the morning and returns at half-past six in the evening, leaving the home in the care of a maid and a nurse whom she supervises. The home is tidy and tastefully furnished; there are six rooms. John and his little sister sleep in the same room but have separate beds. The nurse sleeps in the same room with the children."

The training in this case seems to have been largely in the hands of nurses, but when a child is rebellious he disregards his nurse because he knows she is paid. Children are quick to sense the difference between parents and servants. Our John has perhaps always been able to dominate the nurse, and now he wants to dominate the entire household.

> "John's birth was normal; weight, seven and one-half pounds at birth. He was fed on the bottle from the beginning. He has had German measles, diphtheria, and mumps. Tonsils have been removed. He was taken to one of the neurological hospitals because he fatigued easily, was nervous and had poor muscle control."

There are some medical questions involved here. Although being fed on the bottle is not the best way to bring up a baby, I have seen bottle-fed children who have developed satisfactorily. Anemic, undernourished children frequently have poor muscle control and are easily fatigued, but I hardly think this is the case with John. There is a certain type of fatigue in children and adults which appears more or less as a defense against the demands of their life. I am inclined to believe that this is the reason for his lack of interest in work and play. He does not seem to tire so easily in the conflict with his mother.

> "John does not seem to remember things at the right time. He is always slow in dressing."

Children whose social feeling is not developed do not pay attention or concentrate because they refuse to cooperate, and a defective memory is the result of lack of interest in others. The second point is surely evidence that he is a spoiled child. Only children of this type make problems of dressing, eating, and the like. It may be that he was indulged by one of his so-called strict nurses, and then later severely disciplined. The change in nurses might be sufficient to make a rebel out of him.

> "He dawdles when dressing, and someone must help him to finish on time. He often is late to school because of his slow dressing or because he stops at news stands and reads the headlines. He is

fatigued in the morning, although he goes to bed at nine o'clock."

If John wanted to get to school on time he would dress quickly enough, but school is a problem he does not want to face. He is looking for situations in which he can rule, and school is not one of them. Now, rising in the morning means, "I have to go to school," and we find him hesitating and being tired because these are the best expressions of his disinclination to face reality.

"He says he likes his father as well as his mother."

I do not believe this. If you ask a child, "Whom do you prefer, your mother or your father?" he will answer, "I like both." Children are usually drilled to say this. Even if they are not drilled but are intelligent, they know that it is not nice to express a dislike for one parent. If you really want to know which one the child prefers, don't ask questions, but watch the child's behavior.

"He obeys only his father, who is strict with him; he does not obey anyone else. His mother is too lenient with him and spoils him. She begs him to be good in school every day, but he pays no attention."

The mother's begging is entirely useless, as are tears and outbreaks of temper. This child's goal is fixed, and it is his pattern to avoid all situations in which he is not especially favored. His greatest difficulty is remaining in a situation which he does not dominate. The mother's begging and crying will do no good. The more the child is pushed into an unpleasant situation, the more he pushes back. Sometimes children seem to be prevailed upon to move forward, but defeat always follows, because the child's real goal does not coincide with the behavior which is forced upon him.

> "The mother says he knows that he can do as he likes with her, and is very disobedient and mischievous when left alone with her. He likes to play with his sister, but he does not like the nurse, upon whom he sometimes plays mean tricks. Last week he discharged his water pistol into her mouth. His father punished him by not allowing him to have the pistol at bedtime. He thinks all life is fun."

The surest index of a child's social feeling is to be found in his relation toward servants. We also see that he does not take life seriously. This is quite appropriate to the behavior pattern of a spoiled child. I remember another case which demonstrated this feature to an even more marked degree. A certain boy was always joking and laughing in school, no matter what happened. When the teacher asked him a question, he laughed and could not answer. The teacher thought he was feeble-minded and brought him to me, but when I won his confidence, he talked to me freely and said: "I know they want to fool me; school is established by parents to fool the children." Children should not be ridiculed. In the case just mentioned, the boy's attitude was derived from parents who ridiculed him from early childhood. He was a belligerent child, and when the parents wanted him to be serious, he refused. This type of individual may commit suicide later in life when he finds that the world is not all fun.

> "John wants to play all the time and to be silly when in school. He wants to annoy and bother the teacher. He has no feeling of responsibility and no feeling for the rights of others. He has no friends in his class."

Now you see what a well-developed technique this child has acquired to avoid the responsibilities and duties of a classroom and at the same time maintain the center of attention. Really, when we understand his pattern of life, we must admit that it is very intelligent of him not to have a feeling of responsibility or any interest in the rights of others. If I were to hear that John liked to go to school in the face of all the facts in his history, I should suspect his mentality.

> "His classmates look upon him as a great nuisance. He is always annoying, pushing, and stepping on others. He delights in tripping up other children or fighting with any child he is near. I always had him sitting next to my desk. I always

had him the first in line so I could control his actions. He goes down-stairs so badly that I am always afraid he will trip and fall and perhaps hurt someone. He seems to have poor muscular control."

It is quite evident from this report that John has won his point and considers himself the conqueror of the teacher. I have often seen very spoiled children who have made trouble in the line, but I have seldom seen one who was so spoiled that he could not keep his balance. Perhaps John is playing the rôle of a clumsy child to make others laugh. On the other hand, there are children who do not walk correctly because no one has understood how to train them to function for themselves, and the children themselves have not been interested in learning because dependence fitted into their pattern.

"The friends with whom he plays on the street are five boys he met at camp."

I wonder whether he has poor muscular control when he is playing or fighting on the street. As he has developed in the pattern of an only child, I should expect him to prefer the company of older boys. This is not always true, but only children are usually to be found in the company of older persons. You might think this strange courage in a boy who has evaded most problems, but I believe that if he goes with older boys, he does so because he is sure they will not attack him.

> "He is always fighting with other boys who come around his block. He likes fighting better than anything else and always blames it on the others. He fights so much with schoolboys that he must be kept at home until ten minutes before school opens in the afternoon because of the many complaints that have been registered by other parents. He likes to play cops and robbers and other street games."

This is not so much courage as a cheap imitation of heroism.

> "He likes mystery stories where detectives catch robbers. He reads a great deal, very quickly, preferring ghost stories and mystery tales. He does not belong to any club."

Surely we have had enough evidence now to assert that this is a mismanaged child whose pattern is directed to maintain the center of attention by fair means or foul.

> "He has been to camp since the age of five and one-half and he likes sports. He was so mischievous that the camp director wanted to send him home, but the counselor liked his intellect and pleaded to keep him, chiefly because of his innocent tone of voice. Each year the counselor helped

him with making his bed, cleaning his tent, and so on. He is untidy, late and disobedient at camp, but he manages to evade responsibility wherever he goes."

I am in great favor of camps for children, but I must say that you cannot expect a camp to change a child's life pattern if it is already well established. If there is someone at the camp who thoroughly understands the child, such a change may be effected, but it is foolish to belief that a child's bad behavior will necessarily be improved by camp life. John attained his goal of useless superiority and parasitism even in the camp, by the development of such undesirable traits as slyness and feigned innocence.

"He shows very superior general intelligence and prefers working problems in arithmetic. He likes school work and does not object to any studies that he can master."

These are excellent reports. Probably he has had success in arithmetic and therefore has been interested in making progress in it. I believe we can solve his problem if we indulge him correctly, and thus make him interested in worth-while things. We know this is not the proper way to handle the situation later on, but we must begin by winning him over to our way of thinking. He is not guilty, because he has no idea that his main interest in life is to evade responsibility.

"Mentally he is about a year in advance of his physical age. In 1A he liked his teacher and got along very well with his lessons; his conduct was B and work A. After one month he was promoted to 1B; in 1B he disliked his teacher and his conduct was D and his work B. In 2A the conduct was C, the work A; in 2B, the conduct D, the work A; in 3B his work fell off; conduct D, work C. His best subjects are reading and arithmetic. His poorest subject is physical training, although he tested ten years on a muscle-coordination test."

The fact that there seem to be no organic reasons for his poor coordination justifies us in our belief that he plays the rôle of a clumsy child because he is not especially interested in physical exercise. He was probably criticized in the gymnasium.

"He fatigues easily and must lie down after some classes. He is not allowed to use ink in penmanship as he gets it all over himself; his papers are very untidy, his drawing is poor."

It may be that his fatigue after classes is a sort of joke he is playing on the teacher.

"He was continually sent to the principal's office because of his disturbing conduct in class. The principal said it was too bad John could not smile and that he had such a sad expression. This sad expression is his way of trying to appear innocent."

If sending John to the principal two or three times did not have the desired effect, it should have been discontinued. Smiling may be the expression of various emotions, and perhaps it is too much to expect many smiles from this particular rebel. His rôle is that of an innocent person accused by mistake.

> "When scolded for any misbehavior he assumes a mild, babyish voice. He continues talking a great deal about it and hardly stops for breath. He never wants for an excuse to fit the deed, and often lies to excuse himself."

By talking continually, he probably hopes to defeat his superiors. His slyness is the result of trying to evade his father's discipline.

> "The boy was sent to be examined by the psychologists at one of the universities in January, 1928. This is the summary of the results. 'Physical: height and weight above normal; vision impaired but helped by glasses; dental care needed. Mental age ten years and three months; motor coordination and perception of relationships at ten-year level; comprehension, 4A level; comprehension of arithmetic, 5A level.' "

This examination gives us a hint that the boy is suffering from some organic defects, and through lack of encouragement, has refused to make proper compensation.

"The father insists that John come in from the street at five o'clock, but John disobeys and does not come in promptly. His gang have a rule that anyonc who leaves before a closed session of the day is announced, receives sixty punches. Of course, John would prefer hitting others, to being hit himself, and therefore stays over his allotted time. He does not remember the things that he is told to do by his parents. His father cannot understand this, because John is very intelligent. John's friends get a fifty-cent allowance, and John wants the same. His parents do not believe that he needs so much money, as they give him everything he needs at home and they do not want him to abuse money. John's friends used to go to Sunday school with him, but now they have decided to stay away, and John wants to stay away also. His parents insist that he attend religious instruction."

These facts indicate that John is much happier with his gang where he plays an important rôle. He does not remember to obey his parents because their demands do not fit into his pattern.

"The father is very anxious for John to get good marks in conduct. He brings home a conduct card every day, and the father bribes him to be good. He has organized a system of cash payments for good behavior. If John gets B he gets fifteen cents, B plus, twenty cents, A, twenty-five cents. But if John gets C he pays his father ten cents, and if he gets D, twenty-five cents. Recently John brought home a D in conduct; his father scolded him and gave him a slight taste of how the rolling-pin felt by administering a few light taps and promised him a severe whipping if he got a D again. Unfortunately, John returned that very day with another D."

The father, for all his good intentions, is only working on the surface. It is impossible to bribe a boy to be good, if his pattern demands non-conformity. And it must be evident to everyone that, for this child, corporal punishment is worse than useless.

"In school his lessons are very good, but his conduct is very annoying. He disturbs the class work by talking to himself and to other children and by playing the clown to attract attention. His desk is kept in a very untidy state, with some of his books on the seat, some on the floor, and papers strewn all around. His written work is very untidy, as is his personal appearance at the end of the day, although he is clean and neat when he comes in the morning. The father of another boy in his class came to school with the following complaint: John had threatened to fight his son and had planned to meet him on a certain corner after school. The boy was afraid to go to school, for fear John would attack him. The children in his class do not like him because he always wants to be the leader and will allow no one else to assume any authority."

These are further corroborations of the pattern that we have seen worked out before. If the boy is an excellent fighter, there can hardly be a poor coordination of his muscles.

"The boy usually plays on the street until five o'clock when he goes to his father's shop, remaining until six, and returns home for supper. Reads in the kitchen until the nurse says his baby sister is asleep, and then goes to bed at nine o'clock. On rainy days, he goes to his father's shop and reads a book."

Perhaps one of the reasons for his reading is that he dislikes reality and prefers to indulge himself in fantasies in which he is identified with the heroes of his books.

"The home training and discipline have been very inadequate; both parents have spoiled him. He has been left to himself after school hours and allowed to get into bad habits. He seems to be acquiring the gang spirit. He is not afraid in the dark nor does he call out in his sleep, but he is very restless in bed."

John's fearlessness in the dark is a mistake, for he could easily force his mother or the nurse to pay attention to him during the night as well as the day.

> "He wants to be a detective so he can catch robbers, or a doctor so he can cure people of cancer (his grandfather died of cancer), or a lawyer so he can help people in trouble."

In these days the cure of cancer is a heroic deed. As he has described his ambitions it seems as though he had a certain degree of social feeling which fits into the picture of his gang activities. Street boys have a certain honest tradition: they are faithful to one another; and the fact that he belongs to a gang may be very beneficial to him. That he prefers to be a detective, rather than a robber, is also reassuring. John's record is not entirely black, and there are certain good phases in his development. The chief difficulty is that he has misplaced his emphasis. He fights because it is the only way he knows to gain significance. From this point we must proceed in the therapy. We shall speak to the parents, and advise the father not to whip him, but to make a companion of him. It would be a good thing for them to take a trip together and try to understand each other.

It is of the greatest importance to make the boy and the parents realize that John's goal is to gain attention. It will be more difficult with the boy, and it may take some time before we can convince him about his own aim in life. We must use every means at our command to help him. Fortunately, we have his teacher here, and I know that she will help very much to explain the boy's behavior to him and direct him in a better way.

## Conference

STUDENT. If this child's goal is in his unconscious, how can he be rational about it?

DR. ADLER. We proceed by holding up a mirror to his soul; we enable him to see his attitude and compare it with other pictures that we make. If we are successful in making him see himself as he actually is, the time will come when he will think of this while he is misbehaving, and his procedure will be weakened. And once he has completely understood the reasons for his behavior, he will be a different boy.

The mother and father enter the room.

DR. ADLER. We have taken some pains to try to understand your boy, John, and I believe we have been successful. It seems to me that if you will do your share, we can help you to make him a normal child. It appears that John's chief goal in life is to gain attention. Sometimes he does this in a constructive way, sometimes in a bad way. He has made good progress in reading and arithmetic, and his behavior toward his younger sister is reassuring, as is his ambition to be a useful person later in life. But his bad behavior is an indication that the boy feels injured and discriminated against. We should like to know more about his childhood situation. If a child is first overindulged and petted, and then suddenly loses his accustomed support, he feels as though he had lost a paradise. He may spend the rest of his life avoiding any situation of which he is not the master. If he does not get the center of attention without effort, as he did in his coddled babyhood, he develops the personality of a rebel and fights for it. He will fight his mother, his teacher, other children, as long as he is not the most admired and the strongest individual in the situation. John is struggling to reconquer the paradise which he believes he has lost. Now the history says that he had a very strict nurse for the first sixteen months. Is this so?

MOTHER. She was always strict. She never allowed anyone to go near the baby.

DR. ADLER. Do you remember whether he liked her?

MOTHER. He was too young to understand at the time.

DR. ADLER. Was the second nurse more strict than the other?

MOTHER. I think she was nicer to him.

DR. ADLER. It seems impossible to reconstruct the circumstances exactly, but it is probable that this boy was babied by a nurse, by a maid, or by you. You see, he was an only child for a number of years. Did you spoil him?

MOTHER. No, I never did.

Dr. Adler. Then we must presume it was a nurse. But whoever it was, we know that his situation suddenly changed. How long has John been giving you trouble?

Mother. For two years. He had a little trouble in the beginning of school but has been worse since the age of seven.

Dr. Adler. It often happens that a child's difficulties begin when he enters school, where he cannot maintain his position of effortless superiority.

Mother. He went to a private school at first, where he had a great deal of freedom.

Dr. Adler. Probably he felt that the change to the new school shifted him from a favorable to an unfavorable situation. John's behavior is intelligent, but he is mistaken in his goal. The boy will never change until we convince him that he can only be loved and appreciated by being useful. I suggest that you both make an effort to show him that you are really his friends. If you can win him over to this point of view, his disobedience will disappear. I am sure that he can be reconciled to his place in the family, as well as to his place in the school. Taking him to the principal, giving him bad reports, spanking him, bribing him with money, do not work. I suggest that you try my method, and if you like I shall say a few words to John and explain to him that he is not a bad boy, but that you have all misunderstood each other.

Mother. Yes.

DR. ADLER. Thank you, I will speak to him.

Parents leave the room.

DR. ADLER. The father looked very doubtful when I suggested that the boy could be helped. This does not matter. If you make suggestions to parents in an audience like this, and they say "No," do not antagonize them by insisting on your point of view, but let them go. Frequently their refusal changes to acquiescence after they have left the room. It was my chief desire to point out to his parents that John is not guilty, because they have always considered him so. We have overlooked one point—their insistence that he go to Sunday school. You see that by their strictness they cause him to rebel against religion also. A child always chooses the things that the parents overvalue as the point of attack against them. If a boy is good in reading and arithmetic, and can fight, I am certain that he can also do well in other subjects and conduct himself perfectly.

The boy comes in.

DR. ADLER. I hear that you want to be a doctor, as I am. Would you like it?

JOHN. Yes.

DR. ADLER. It is very interesting to help other people out of their difficulties. It is really easy, otherwise we would not have so many doctors. Have you many friends?

JOHN. Yes.

DR. ADLER. Very good friends?

JOHN. Yes.

DR. ADLER. And do you like them?

JOHN. Yes.

DR. ADLER. That is fine. Are you the leader?

JOHN. We take turns being the leader.

DR. ADLER. Would you like to be the leader always? It is splendid to be a leader in good work, but sometimes a boy believes it is better to be a leader in bad things. It takes a great deal of courage to be a leader in good things. It seems to me that you always like to be the center of attention. Did they spoil you when you were a child?

JOHN. No.

DR. ADLER. Suppose you think it over. Perhaps you feel you are not made as much of as you used to be and feel that the only way you can attract notice is to disturb your class or quarrel with your mother. Perhaps you have not found any other way, but I am sure that a boy as clever as you are could do it better. Are you courageous enough to try a new way? I know that you can accomplish anything you like and I am sure that you could be one of the best pupils in your school. Perhaps you do not believe it and are afraid to try. Don't you think it would be much more pleasant if everybody said, "John is a fine boy"? To disturb people in order to be the center of attention is very cowardly. It is much braver to help other people. Are you brave enough to try it? How long do you think it will take you to become one of the best-behaved pupils in the class? I feel sure that you are bright enough to do it in two weeks. Will you come and see me again in two weeks and tell me how you are getting along?

JOHN. Yes.

## *THE FEAR OF GROWING UP*

THIS evening we will consider the case of George, a boy six years and eight months old, in the 1B grade. The case history states that the mother is bringing him here in the hope that we can help to correct his speech defect. He talks baby talk and has other bad habits, such as grimacing, clowning, and pretending not to be able to read or answer questions. His intelligence quotient is 89. It is possible that his peculiarities of speech are due to an organic defect. But as the child has other bad habits, it is more likely that he is badly adjusted in some way. If the latter is true, the child speaks improperly either to avoid associations with his fellows or to narrow them to a sphere in which he feels himself secure. We must corroborate our hypothesis with other evidence. He may be untidy, unsocial, a food faddist, a timid child, and so on. With an I.Q. of 89, he is undoubtedly intelligent and therefore there must be a purpose in his acting like a baby. From former experiences, I suspect that this is a child who is afraid to face the problem of growing up. I know of a five-year-old boy who always wanted to drink out of a bottle. In this very obvious manner he insisted on fixing himself in the favorable situation of infancy. He had an inferiority complex. Such a child does not say in so many words, "I do not want to grow up," but he acts correctly to avoid a new condition which he does not understand. Even if the child knew consciously that he did not want to grow up, he would still be unconscious of the reasons for his reluctance. Consciousness and unconsciousness are never contradictions. They are two streams that flow in the same direction.

A child who wants to remain a baby will almost inevitably have bad habits. It is very important to know why he has chosen this goal. Perhaps he has been badly spoiled, perhaps he was a handsome baby, perhaps he was sick in the beginning of his life, or perhaps he is an only boy or the youngest child. His clowning and making faces, which are excellent ways to get attention, confirm the impression that he is a spoiled child, and that he is fighting for the pleasurable condition which he feels is slipping away from him. His baby talk is not a defect but a stroke of genius. Baby talk and grimaces are part of the marvelous creative work of the child. Grant that he wants to remain a baby, and you can find no more effective technique than the one he has chosen. Many children find a way to be comical. Sometimes they are laughed at for something they have done accidentally and then practice similar activities until they really become artists in making themselves ridiculous.

By pretending not to read George makes other people work for him and projects himself back into babyhood when he was not expected either to read or to answer questions. It would be a great mistake to reproach him or punish him for his tricks. He is not lying, because he is pursuing his own goal—not the one his parents have set for him. If it were his goal in life to be a good pupil, he would learn to read and to answer questions. Instead he pretends, "I cannot." When we translate this into our psychological language it means, "I am a baby, you must expect nothing of me."

The case history says:

> "His family consists of a brother fourteen years old and two sisters, eleven and nine years old."

This is the second corroboration of our hypothesis. As the youngest child he is very likely to be spoiled.

> "The brothers and sisters quarrel with George very often."

This is interesting because it shows that George is not entirely cowardly. The older children would hardly quarrel with him if he had lost all his courage.

> "He gets along better with his sisters, especially the eleven-year-old one. The older sister is a very capable child and during the mother's illness took her place in the household."

Evidently the older sister gives him the sort of attention he wants. The mother probably spoiled him first, and the sister occasionally imitates her.

> "The older brother hits George, objects to his friends, especially a little colored boy whom George brings home. He says George has terrible manners."

These "terrible manners" are the manners of a baby. I do not find them terrible; I think they are very artistic. If he is going to act like a baby, he must defend himself like one. He cannot change his goal, because he has no insight into his situation. I hardly believe it will be very difficult to make George understand that to grow up means to have more power, and that it is better to strive for progress than to look for the paradise of the past.

This gives us an indication of the value of school, for George will have an open road to the future if his teacher can encourage and train him in the art of growing up. His mother also must be persuaded to make him more independent, and urge him to take more interest in other members of the family and in his playmates. The older boy must be taught that his methods are wrong. None of the children should laugh when he makes grimaces. They should not give him the opportunity to make himself important by such cheap tricks.

> "The other children in the family hate to hear George's baby talk. The older brother and sister do very good work in school, and both are in a high I.Q. group. The younger sister is in a low I.Q. group. George is a handsome blond boy, and the others are dark and not at all attractive. The mother says, " 'We could not help loving him; he was so blond and cute.' "

Here are more and more corroborations of our theory that he is a pampered child.

> "The father is an Italian, a bricklayer. The mother is an American. The parents are not happy together."

This is a complicating factor in the child's development. If the parents are not happy together and the boy leans too much on his mother, his tendency is probably to exclude his father from his love. This narrows his life too much, and is a reason for his wanting to remain an irresponsible baby.

> "George came to school one day very much upset and said, 'Mother did not come home all night; my daddy made mamma cry and she went out and did not come back.' It worried him all morning and he kept asking me whether it wasn't time to go home."

The quarrel in this family must be a very bitter one if the mother stays out all night. Under such circumstances it is particularly difficult for a child to develop any social feeling. Evidently he is deeply attached to his mother.

> "When the mother came home, she told him that she had been to the movies and became so ill that she could not come home."

This is an indication that the mother lies to the child, and, while I should not advise her to tell the child the entire truth, I am sure she could find a less transparent lie.

> "At one time the family was very comfortably situated, owned property and an automobile in the South. The mother is sorry that they left the South. She was very ill for a long time, and the father was out of work for months. A few months ago he appealed to the school for financial aid, but now he is working."

Here is another difficulty in this child's case. The boy probably remembers that his childhood was considerably happier than his present condition because the family had more money and less worry.

> "The mother has a sixteen-year-old nephew living in another state who has a speech defect similar to George's."

This makes me think that the mother believes in inheritance. The mother of this other boy is a sister of

George's mother, and they both have come from a family that spoiled its children. This is not a matter of inheritance, but a set of similar circumstances. We must never leave a family tradition out of our inquiry, but when we investigate thoroughly we frequently find that the supposed inheritance of character traits is merely ignorant superstition.

> "The child's birth was normal, but he was a very difficult child to feed and was often sick until he was three years old."

Perhaps this child has a defective alimentary tract, or perhaps his mother was simply not skilful in feeding him. It is very likely he was pampered while he was sick, because that is in accordance with this family tradition.

> "He has had an operation for the removal of his tonsils, as the parents believed it would help his speech, but it had no effect."

Naturally his situation was not changed by a tonsillectomy. If a boy wants to be a baby, he will be a baby with or without tonsils.

> "The doctors have assured the mother that there is nothing wrong with his speech organs. The school doctor finds that, aside from a few carious teeth, he is in good condition. At school the other children like him and enjoy his grimaces."

Young school children are easily pleased and George has trained himself to be amusing.

> "He often gets into fights with his classmates, pushing them, or talking to children who sit near him. He comes to school looking clean, but soon pulls his stockings down over his shoes and opens his tie."

These are all tricks of his repertoire as an actor.

> "He never hangs his coat up but just throws it into the closet. He came to school on cold days without a coat because he said his winter coat was too short for him, and he refused to wear his lumber jacket because it had a hole in it."

Untidiness is an unmistakable sign of a spoiled child, but George is also vain and does not want to appear badly dressed. Perhaps the fact that he used to have nice clothes when his parents were better off is an important factor in his life. If he always had had a coat with a hole in it, he would not know the difference.

> "His work in arithmetic is good and he is learning to read nicely."

These are good signs that he is overcoming the difficulties of school, and evidently he has a kind teacher, or he would be likely to have trouble with arithmetic.

"His writing is very poor, and his papers are untidy and dirty."

This point leads us to believe that he might be left-handed, in which case writing would be specially hard for him.

"He is a converted left-hander. He never attempts to use his left hand in the classroom, but he can write numbers quite well with his left hand."

We were right in our assumption that he is a left-handed child, and that he has not completely compensated for the weakness of his right hand in writing. Frequently such children have difficulty in learning how to read and are considered stupid because of their failure, but if we investigate closely we find that they can read quite well from right to left—mirror-writing.

"He responds quickly to praise."

This hardly needs an interpretation.

"He is not clumsy but pretends to be unable to do things. For instance, if the teacher is watching him he pretends that he cannot fold his paper, but if she does not look at him, he can do it perfectly."

Over and over again we see this boy's goal in life; to make everyone who is kind to him do his bidding. He is trying to prove that he is only a baby.

> "He does not dress himself; he hates to be washed, and when his mother washes him he makes a terrible fuss and screams with all his might."

More signs that he has been spoiled. He screams when his mother washes him, not because he dislikes being washed, but because he wants to give her more trouble.

> "She punishes him by whipping and sometimes, to avoid the fuss, she rewards the eleven-year-old sister for washing him. He feeds himself, but very slowly and with much playing."

No mother who has overindulged her son in other ways will be able to impress him with the necessity of washing himself, merely by whipping him. Meal times are evidently turned into opportunities for him to attract more attention.

> "He is not obedient at home; often makes the same faces at home that he makes at school, and never puts his toys or clothes away. He sleeps in the same bed with his nine-year-old sister and the older sister sleeps in the same room."

The mother should be told that the sleeping arrangements are not the best that might be made.

> "The father does not punish him at all, but the relation between mother and son is much stronger

than between father and son. Mother said she would feel 'terrible' if he preferred his father."

This throws a great deal of light upon our case. It was apparent that the bond was closer between the mother and the child, but it seems that she has actually prevented the child from companionship with his father. Even though the mother had not made this statement we might have come to the same conclusion. For if the marriage is an unhappy one, and the child inclines toward the mother, the mother unconsciously and instinctively makes him a partizan against the father.

"He plays with some boys on the street, but prefers playing with girls."

Such a preference fits into his pattern. He prefers women because he has been indulged by his mother and his older sister. If it was necessary to find a tutor for him, this point would be one to consider. To be sure, it is not wise to allow a child to remain in this mistaken emotional fixation, but we must remember that in the beginning we cannot attack him too strenuously. I should say if he needed a tutor, he should have a woman.

"It is his ambition to grow up to be a cowboy, because the cowboys he sees in the movies all fight."

It is very common for disheartened children to play a heroic rôle in their fantasies. To this boy being a cowboy is an approximation of godlikeness. It should not be too difficult to get this boy to forge ahead. His ambition shows that he would really like to grow up, if it was made easy for him. In other words, he wants to be a hero under the proper conditions.

> "He dreams that a man comes and takes the door of his house away."

We could almost guess this boy's dreams. The proper dreams for such a child would point to the danger of growing up, and with them he would deceive himself into justifying his desire to remain a baby. Now the dream that is stated in the case history is rather curious, but I think it can be interpreted. If someone came and took the door of the house away, the house would be open and he would not be protected. The door is a protection and George is very much interested in his defenses.

From a sample of his handwriting, there are several indications that he is left-handed. For instance, he reverses his "M's" and has very narrow margins on the left side of the paper. His handwriting is very bad.

The greatest task here is to persuade his mother to reconcile George with his father. The older children should be told not to criticize him and not to pay attention to his grimaces. The mother must try to make him more independent. She can reward him when he washes and dresses himself and runs errands for the family. I believe that the teacher understands the child thoroughly and needs very little instruction. She might wait for the opportunity to praise him when his paper is a little less untidy, and he should not be scolded if his paper is dirty. When he tries to attract attention, the teacher should exaggerate her response. She might tell him personally, and not in the presence of other children, that if he really wants her to, she will do all his work for him. Then she should say something like this: "You see, your mother has spoiled you a little, and so you always want to have somebody working for you and taking care of you. This is a poor way to grow up to be a man. It is good only if you want to remain a baby."

### Conference

The boy, George, comes in with his mother, holding on to her, and will not shake hands with Dr. Adler.

Dr. Adler. Why won't you shake hands with me? I am your friend. I see you are a big boy and you ought to be able to walk alone without your mother. You are not a baby, are you?

The boy walks away from the mother with Adler.

Dr. Adler. Have you many friends? Are they good friends? Do you help them?

George nods his head in assent to all these questions but does not look at Dr. Adler.

Dr. Adler. You see, he is not sure that I am his

friend, and he will not look at me. (To George) You think I am going to bite you? What do you like to do most of all?

GEORGE. Paint.

DR. ADLER. Would you like to be a painter?

George does not answer.

DR. ADLER. What would you like better than being a painter?

GEORGE. I would like to be a cowboy.

DR. ADLER. What would you do if you were a cowboy?

GEORGE. I would ride horseback.

DR. ADLER. You don't have to be a cowboy to ride horseback. I am sure you can do anything you want to. Tell me, would you like to be a baby? Or would you rather be a teacher, or a doctor?

George answers "No" to these questions.

DR. ADLER. I think that if you were more careful with your school work and kept your hands clean, people would like you better, and your teacher would praise you. Is your brother rough with you? I am going to tell him not to fight with you any more. I shall also tell him not to listen to you if you talk like a baby. From now on, if you make faces like a baby nobody will look at you, and you can make them all day and all night if you like. What are you going to do when you grow older? Wouldn't you like to learn to speak and recite very well?

GEORGE. Yes.

Dr. Adler. Then you must begin to dress and wash yourself, and eat correctly and not be a baby any more. How can you be a cowboy if you act like a baby all the time? That is not the right way to train yourself.

The boy hurries away.

Dr. Adler. His quick exit indicates that he is not comfortable in the presence of people, but I believe we have put a new idea into his head.

Dr. Adler (to the mother). George has created the rôle of a baby for himself, probably because he remembers that, as a small child, he was in a very pleasant situation and he wishes to restore it. For this reason he makes trouble for you, forces you to wash and dress him, and to keep him a baby. He does not want to be naughty; he is a good pupil and a fine boy, and I am sure he will overcome his difficulties in a short time. If you want to help, do not notice his grimaces and do not reproach him for them. See that the other children ignore him when he makes faces. When he talks baby talk act as if you did not hear him, and praise him when he speaks like a grown-up boy. He leans on you too much and is too shy with others. It would be a good thing if his brother and father would make an effort to be friendly with him. I know that he is being properly encouraged at school and if you help him, too, everything will go well. Let him wash and dress himself, even if it takes a long time. When you see him making an effort in the right direction, praise him and say, "I am glad you are a grown-up boy now and no longer a baby." All his bad habits are caused by the fact that he is afraid to grow up, and he must be encouraged to understand that it is not really dangerous. Do not preach to him, but when he talks like a baby, pay no attention to him until he tries to speak correctly.

The mother agrees to carry out the instructions.

DR. ADLER (to students). You see, sometimes I do not give many direct instructions, because no one can tell a mother all the little tricks that are necessary to cure such a child, but if she understands the total situation she will know what to do. It is impossible to give a set of rules which will cover every emergency. Of course, this family seems rather unhappy, but, occasionally, a few small changes in the household will clear up the whole atmosphere.

STUDENT. How can you love a child without indulging him?

DR. ADLER. You can love a child all you wish, but you must not make him dependent. You owe it to the child to let him function as an independent being, and you must begin training him from the very beginning to do this. If a child gains the impression that his parents have nothing to do but to be at his beck and call, he gains a false idea of love.

## *THE REBELLIOUS "BAD" BOY*

THIS evening we have the case of a boy twelve years and five months of age, whose present problem is that he is incorrigible. He is accused of fighting, and stealing while on probation, and the parents have been advised to send him away to an institution.

This arrangement probably means that the parents have not found the way to persuade this child to live a correct life. No doubt there are cases in which every person, even one who has been well trained in individual psychology, feels that he is incapable of changing a child's pattern of life, but we must never despair of finding a correct method nor doubt that another person can do it if we cannot. In very difficult cases, it is sometimes wise to speak to the problem child or adult in this way: "I believe I know why you act like this but I do not know whether I can make you see it as clearly as I do." This usually makes a good impression upon the patient. Children and adults of this type are suffering from inferiority and superiority complexes, and if they find a teacher or a doctor who is not conceited enough to think he can cure any case, or does not suffer when he has to admit a failure it is a great relief to the patients, especially to a child who believes he must show that no teacher can succeed with him. If you approach such a child with the attitude, "Perhaps I will not succeed, but another person could," you soften his antagonism.

It is to be expected that a belligerent child of this type would also be accused of fighting and stealing. He feels cheated and yet he is courageous enough to fight for his rights—probably against a weak environment. The case history tells us that he has been on probation. Being on probation is in itself a bad thing, and it is a pity that we did not see this boy four or five years earlier, before probation was begun. At the present time the boy is branded because he is on probation. The fact that the parents have been advised to send him away indicates that his environment has exhausted its resources, has become hopeless about his future, and labeled him an incorrigible boy. Under the circumstances I should not be against sending him away, but where shall we send him? Who will understand this boy and train him for a useful life? It is essential that this child be made self-confident, that he like his teacher or the doctor who tries to help him. I do not know where we could send him to have this done, but I do know that if there were a mental-hygiene clinic in his school, the problem could be attacked there advantageously. In the mental-hygiene clinic some friend or tutor would be found for him, who would allow him to experience a human fellowship which he has not found in his home. The usual thing is to send such a boy to a reformatory, but it has been my observation that most young criminals have been to reformatories. I very much doubt whether anyone has ever been reformed by a reformatory.

Let us turn to the case notes:

> "Past problems are: difficulties in school, stealing and fighting. He was sent to a parental home for three months."

No doubt his commitment to the parental home simply exaggerated this child's protest.

> "The family is German. The father, who was a strict, stern man, and preferred the oldest girl in the family, died of tuberculosis. The mother is much older than her second husband. The stepfather is very friendly with Nicholas. A sister died at the age of six years. She was two years older than Nicholas. Another sister, thirteen months older than the patient, is alive. He has a half-sister now, four years old. Nicholas was four years and four months old when the oldest sister died, and four years and six months old when the father died.

Apparently the father was not the sort of person who would have fostered Nicholas's social feelings. We must look for the impression that the deaths in his family had upon him. The half-sister is eight years younger and is probably no rival to him. His style of life had been fixed and established before she was born. We can hazard the guess, therefore, that the person in his environment who makes difficulties for him is his older sister, and we can presume that she has developed very well, is a good girl, and is preferred by the mother. If the evidence confirms this inference we can easily understand the dynamics of his life. He feels that he has been discriminated against and is afraid that he cannot compete. Probably he has been discouraged because he has not found a good method to surpass his sister.

> "The father and the mother do not complain of any difficulties between each other. Nicholas and his oldest sister quarrel constantly. His stepfather is good to him and tries to win his confidence. Nicholas is very fond of his half-sister. The mother says she cannot endure Nicholas any longer and wants him sent away because he is noisy and gets the house dirty."

These are very significant facts. Our presumption that rivalry exists between Nicholas and his older sister has been confirmed. The stepfather seems to be a well-meaning man, but his method of reconciling Nicholas is inadequate. As we suspected, the youngest daughter is not a rival. There is conflict between the mother and our patient, and we may be certain from the tone of her remarks about him that her relations with the boy are not good. We know that Nicholas wants to surpass his older sister, but finds her too strong. He expects his mother to promote his interests, and when she refuses he attacks her by being untidy and by fighting. He expresses his discouragement by stealing. He has chosen his mother's weak point by being noisy and dirty—although most twelve-year-old boys are noisy and dirty.

> "The stepfather owns a meat market. The mother receives a small pension and keeps house for the family. The family circumstances are moderate. They have a five-room apartment, the parents having a bedroom to themselves, while the two girls sleep together and Nicholas sleeps on a couch in the dining-room. Nicholas attends a Methodist Sunday school.
>
> "His birth was normal and he was a good baby. He was weaned at five and one-half months and was noticeably undersized until he was ten years old. He walked at thirteen months, talked at sixteen months. At the present time he masturbates."

These undersized children are frequently very aggressive, and in Nicholas's case the fact that he was small might have been a considerable stimulus to competition with his older sister. It is my opinion that masturbation in young and maladjusted children is derived chiefly from their desire to attract notice, as well as their desire to be watched and guarded, and this fits in with our supposition that the patient wants more attention from his mother and probably feels that she cares more for the older sister.

> "He has been examined at the Post Graduate Hospital by a psychiatrist and put on a medication of bromides and pituitary gland. The treatment has been discontinued. The mother says that before the death of the boy's father she had no difficulties with him. The difficulties began much later, when she took him back after her second marriage."

We are almost forced to believe that the mother handled Nicholas very well for the first four years. Then the father's death occurred, the boy was sent away, and after her remarriage she took him back. It is probable that because he deprived him of his mother the stepfather did not succeed in winning over the boy.

The boy could not make an adjustment after he came back, because he came into a new situation for which he was unprepared, and the reason for his difficulty with his mother is that he believed her responsible for his lessened importance.

> "After the father's death the boy was placed in the father's sister-in-law's home for two months. There were two other children in this family, and the foster-mother complained that both Nicholas and his sister were bad, and she wanted more money for keeping them."

Here is a situation in which both children began to fight because they were in an uncongenial environment.

> "Then Nicholas was put into a home with strangers where there were three other children. This family was not clean and did not give Nicholas and his sister enough to eat. Nicholas got into difficulties and mischief with the other children, while going to an outside toilet. Then he was placed with a third family, where the children were never allowed to play outside of the house. The mother often found Nicholas crying on the bed when she went to visit the children. She really wanted to be kind and good to the children, and brought them presents every time she came. An older girl took Nicholas's sister out sometimes, but left Nicholas at home. He remained in this home for a year and a half, until the mother remarried."

The boy has had repeated experiences of humiliation, and he suffered deeply in the first six years of his life.

> "When Nicholas first returned to his home he cried a great deal and sat on his mother's lap most of the time."

We could hardly have a better corroboration of our suppositions of this boy's situation. The child wanted his mother and couldn't find her. And now he is with her his mother wants to send him away again. Nicholas is anxious to win his mother's love and to be close to her.

> "Nicholas says, 'I want to get away from home to some place where no one knows me.' "

One frequently hears such statements from children who are fighting for their rights. It means the same as being dirty or masturbating. He really does not want to be dirty, or leave his home, or masturbate; he does these things in a spirit of revenge. Certain it is that he feels hopeless in his present circumstances, because there is no one whom he can trust.

> "He also says, 'I don't want to go to school any more because the work is too hard for me. I wish I could go back to the parental home; I liked it there.' "

These remarks are familiar indices of the beginning of a criminal career. You see, if a person believes his work is too hard, he feels he has to steal to earn a living, and now this boy is making a gesture of bravado, as if he wanted to be a criminal and wanted to go to jail. Such statements are signs of hopeless rage, and I see that we shall have to gain the boy's confidence before we can do much with him.

> "He rushes into the room in the morning and makes his older sister wait on him. He screams

> for his meals, teases his older sister and, although usually impudent to his mother, he is sometimes affectionate to her. He talks back to his father and is disobedient and refuses to help him."

Here is the whole family drama. By screaming for his meals he says in effect, "I am cheated because you do not take enough care of me." His sister and his father are his enemies, and he is revenging himself on his mother.

> "He steals food in enormous amounts."

This is a point that should be investigated more carefully, to learn whether he eats the food or gives it away to others. Diabetic children often have the desire to steal quantities of food. Such children are always hungry and thirsty and are usually considered nuisances about the house, until someone finds out that they have diabetes.

> "He runs out of the house and does not come back for hours. He says he will run away when he is thirteen years old."

This means, not merely that he prefers to be away from home, but that he wishes to occupy his mother with running after him.

> "He eats disgustingly at the table."

This is a corroboration of the points we have already mentioned.

> "Until three months ago he was kept in a special class at school. He fights with other children and deliberately spoils their games. He also steals from these children and swears at them in vile, abusive language."

We could hardly expect this boy to do well in school, because what he really wants is to be the favorite, and since neither teacher nor children allow him to play as important a rôle as he would like, he finds ways of depreciating and humiliating them. He deprives them, to enrich himself, and by cursing his comrades he maintains an artificial elevation in his own eyes.

> "He wants to go back 'where the children are tougher.' He was superior intellectually to the children in the special class. He is impudent to the teachers, disobedient, unruly, sulky, nervous, impatient, rebellious, argumentative, and defiant. He has no respect for authority, and teachers and principals have always hated him. The first day he went to school he stole a kiddy car, the second day a ball. He has stolen ever since and has even broken into a house with two older boys. He was sent to a parental home because he told the judge he wanted to go there."

Nicholas has unfortunately launched himself upon a criminal career because he has been unable to adjust himself to the demands of the school community. He glories in the punishment that is meted out to him.

Many children who are beaten and spanked say, "It does not hurt me, I want you to beat me." He shows a certain amount of strength in his willingness to suffer in order to maintain his ideal. What he needs is a good comrade, who will know how to keep him from falling any lower.

> "He cut off the tails of two cats with his father's cleaver and he let out a carload of chickens, so he could chase them. He started a parked car, setting it rolling down a hill. Once he stole twenty dollars from a woman's apartment. He has taken many small articles from stores and the like."

All these crimes indicate beyond any doubt that he has no social feeling, either for animals or for human beings, and he will do anything in order to annoy people. From one point of view, of course, the boy is justified in behaving as he does, for his goal is to maintain the center of the stage, and to torture and punish his mother, teacher, and all others who do not favor him.

> "He reads for recreation and occasionally goes to the movies. He has no friends."

In a case of this kind it is perhaps fortunate that he has no friends, because if he could make friends more readily he would surely join a gang where he would be appreciated and accepted.

"He roams around alone, jumping on trucks, riding a long way, and then catching other trucks back. If he meets boys on the street, he stops them, asks them who they are, where they are going, and usually makes derogatory remarks which lead to a fight."

He behaves like a wild street boy, and shows some little courage, but of course this is not the proper training for a useful human being.

"He was given money to join the Boy Scouts, which he immediately spent. His father has given him many playthings, such as a bicycle, musical instrument, and the like. While he was in the special class, he received fair marks, doing well in reading, spelling, and language, but poorly in drawing, music and hand-work. At present he is in the fifth grade where he is doing poor work. He refuses to do his homework unless his mother or sister helps him. He never asks aid of his father. His I.Q. has at various times ranged from eighty-five to one hundred and three."

These points indicate again that he regards his step-father as the conqueror in the home and that he refuses to work except under conditions which he specifies. The wide range of the intelligence quotient shows how very relative the values of intelligence tests are.

"The family complains that he gets into some kind of trouble every day. They are tired of having him dragged in by the police. Neighbors constantly complain about his actions, and everything that happens is blamed on him. His sister says that the boy disgraces her. The patient says that it is too crowded in the home, that his father wants him to do too much work. He hates his home, his school, and the town. The teacher wants him sent back to the special class. Other children in his class taunt him and get him into fights. The principal is trying to be kind to him and attempting to get the boys to cooperate. The teacher is attempting to interest him in sports, but so far he has rejected all advances."

This boy is succeeding excellently in attaining his goal in life—to make trouble for other people; but I see that both principal and teacher are on the right path. Perhaps, if one of the boys in the class could win him over as a friend, the fights would cease.

"He wishes to read and be alone. He says the other boys get in his way. No one knows just how he spends his time except when he comes home at night. One of the teachers took him driving in her car all day, and then to supper with friends of hers, and Nicholas made himself most agreeable and helpful, even helping to set the table for an impromptu supper."

You see how easily he can be disarmed on occasion. But a method must be found which works continually, and not only from time to time.

> "His early recollections are the following: he remembers his father chasing him around the table when he asked for a penny, and seeing his older sister fighting with another girl in the street."

His real father was probably not kind to him if this is his first recollection. The memory of his sister's fighting with other children corroborates his feeling that she is a belligerent girl and is guilty in her quarrels with him.

> "He remembers hiding behind a florist shop because he did not want to go to his father's funeral. He recalls seeing the crematory services and his sister dressed while in her coffin."

This boy has evidently been very much impressed by death, but it is hard to tell whether he was refusing to go to his father's funeral because he was moved by his death or because he wanted to revenge himself. I should not be surprised to discover that this boy wants to be a doctor. Many children who have had experiences with death want to be doctors.

> "He dreams at night, screams, and has night terrors. Sometimes he says he dreams of going to an undertaker and of sitting on a nice, soft bed.

The undertaker says, 'Get off there, that's where I dress dead people.' Then he runs out into a room where there are dead people lying on beds."

His screaming at night is a means to persuade his mother that he hasn't the courage to be alone in the dark without her. The recurrence of the death motive shows how clearly this thought looms in his mind as a possible solution of his problems. After all, the possibilities of a boy who is utterly without hope are only three: wandering, suicide, and crime.

"He sometimes dreams that the small image on the mantel opens its eyes, looks at him, grows bigger and bigger, bursts into flame, and disappears. On some nights he sees men looking into the window but he sees only the tops of their heads and their eyes."

These are interesting dreams, for they show that he thinks he is surrounded by enemies both by day and by night. He trains himself to be frightened so that he can scream and call for his mother, to corroborate his feeling that he is timid and that not even his mother takes care of him.

"He wants to join the army or the navy but he will take any job that is offered to him. He does not want to be a lawyer because they have to study too hard. He says he will never be a butcher or a doctor."

The fact that he says he does not want to be a doctor shows that he has been occupied with the idea to some extent. But finally he finds it ridiculous to think of being a doctor, because he makes no progress in school. He does not want to be a butcher, because it is his stepfather's profession and he hates his stepfather. Perhaps, however, it is because he has overcome his inclination to cruelty. If this boy were to choose a career of crime, I doubt whether he would be a murderer. It is more likely that he would be a burglar.

> "He would like to be a traveling salesman, and see the world."

The teacher's interpretation of the case is as follows:

> "I believe that, although the mother is kind to Nicholas in many ways, she feels he is an affliction on her and is anxious to get rid of him because she is afraid he will destroy her happiness with her husband. She lives in terror lest he become such a problem that the husband will tire of the whole family situation, and feels that she must choose between her child and her husband. Nicholas has promised me that he will not scream for his dinner any more, and has kept his word. He has also promised to report to his father's shop for a week, every afternoon after school, to assist in delivering packages. He did

so for the first day, but after that he failed to appear."

Now we are at the end of the case history and I believe that the teacher's interpretation of the mother's state of mind is entirely correct. We seem to be as well acquainted with Nicholas as if we had known him for a long time. We realize he is in a dangerous position, but we know also that he can be propitiated, because the teacher has been able to make a friend of him. We need to find another friend for this boy, so that his continual quarrels in school will cease. And we must explain to him the fallacy of his belief that his sister is preferred to him. We must tell him why, as a second child, he is very ambitious, and why he cannot pardon his mother because she married again. We must try to persuade the stepfather to be even more helpful and comradely with the boy. The teacher in the school occupies the key position. As I have told you so often it is in the school and by the teacher that crime waves must be stopped. The school must become the center of social progress. It is the logical source of all social reforms. We must try to convince the mother in one interview, making her understand that Nicholas considers himself unappreciated, and that therefore she must not punish him or threaten him with the police, but must give him the feeling that he is an intimate member of the family. The older sister, who is probably not too well adjusted socially, must relinquish her belligerent attitude and her rivalry with Nicholas.

## Conference

The mother enters the room.

Dr. Adler. We wish to speak with you concerning your boy. After our examination of his history we believe that this is not at all a hopeless case. We find that he is an intelligent boy, and if we can discover the mistakes that have been made in his early education, and correct them, he will turn out very well. I am sure that you have tried hard to do this, but you see the boy is also trying very hard to show you that he feels he is being discriminated against. I believe that it would be a good thing to convince him that you love him just as much as you do the older girl, who is a very good pupil and has made good progress. We have found that your son believes his sister has a distinct advantage, and he is hopeless because he feels that he is out of the competition. It is for this reason that he wants to make trouble, and annoys you and your family.

The teacher has understood his case very well and has shown him how to make friends and how to improve his school record, and I believe the same thing can be done at home. You might begin by taking him into your confidence. "Do you know a good book we could buy for your little sister?" "Would you like to have your own room?" "What would you like to have for lunch today?" By doing this, the child will feel of some importance. You must also influence his sister to stop quarreling with him. She must be made to understand that he has lost hope through feeling that his unhappy situation at home cannot be changed because you prefer the other children.

MOTHER. He behaves so badly that nobody likes him.

DR. ADLER. When he came back to your home he probably wanted to have you alone, but he found instead that his older sister and your husband had displaced him. That is when the trouble began. You are a kind mother and probably understood how to make a friend of him in the beginning, while he was with you, but on his return, when the trouble began, you did not understand how to treat him. In your endeavor to have him turn out to be a good boy, you have reproached him too much. If a friend makes a mistake, one should only smile and call it to his attention gently. One should not be annoyed; one should not scold. If you think it will do any good, I will talk to him and explain some of the mistakes that have been made. I shall try to convince him that you like him as much as you like the other children. It is your problem to make the home more attractive to him, and everybody in the family must try to conciliate him. The teacher and I will also help, but you must be patient, for the process will take time. This boy is in a very serious predicament, but we must not let him know it. You must never say to him, "You will come to a bad end." You see, he has lost his courage and only wants to have an easy life. It will be your duty to encourage him to face life more bravely.

The boy comes in.

DR. ADLER. How do you do! Suppose you sit down among these friends and tell us what you like to do most.

NICHOLAS. I want to go to West Point and ride a horse and carry a gun.

DR. ADLER. Couldn't you do that on a ranch or on a farm?

NICHOLAS. No, they have fat horses on a farm.

DR. ADLER. Do you like quick horses, race horses? Are you having a race with your sister, to see who is going to come out ahead?

NICHOLAS. Yes.

DR. ADLER. I believe you are not brave enough. She is a good pupil in school. But it seems to me that you have lost hope of being a good pupil. Your teacher is convinced that you could be a good pupil if you paid more attention to the work. I believe that you are a clever boy and could be one of the best pupils in your class, if you tried. It takes some time though, but it is bound to happen. You cannot go to West Point right away, and it requires a great deal of study to be allowed to enter. The best way to get to West Point is to do your present school tasks courageously. You would be very lonesome at West Point, if you have no friends.

You might begin by making friends at school. You have to be able to do more than fight with your comrades, you must make friends with them.

Perhaps you believe your mother does not love you enough and that your sister does not care for you either. I know that your mother does love you, and I am going to send word to your sister, telling her not to fight with you all the time. If I were you I should become a pal to my father. He is a good, kind man and he is not against you. Your mother likes him very much, and when you grow up you will also find that some girl will love you and will marry you. The fact that your mother loves your father does not mean she has stopped loving you. She also loves your younger and older sisters, and you are just one part of the family. If you would help your mother a little more, your mother and sister would certainly like you better. Now I suggest that in the next week you do things that other people do not like, only two times, and then come back and see me again. Do you think you can succeed?

NICHOLAS. Yes.

## *THE HUNGER STRIKE*

THIS evening we are to consider the case of Betty, a six-year-old girl whose chief problem is difficulty in eating, more or less marked in proportion to her attitude to her surroundings. She shows a particular resentment against food if the situation is not exactly to her liking, which is characteristic of a spoiled child. On the other hand, we must be careful to exclude organic diseases such as tuberculosis, rickets, or infectious diseases in which a child might have a similar lack of appetite. Sometimes two-and-one-half-year-old children have the same symptoms we find in maladjusted children, who, when examined, show definite organic changes and are absolutely right in their disinclination to eat. It is necessary for anyone who deals with children to have some medical experience, and lay psychologists and social workers should be very careful lest they make dangerous mistakes in their diagnoses. However, when we hear that Betty's antipathy to food varies with her attitude toward her environment, we may suspect that it is a psychological rather than a medical problem.

The case notes go on to state:

> "Her condition is particularly unfavorable with her mother. Rarely is the child eager for food and almost always she dawdles over her meals. When she eats she keeps a few bolts of food in her cheek and appears agonized at the necessity of swallowing."

This is almost unmistakable evidence that Betty wishes to intensify her dependency on her mother's care. Perhaps her mother spoiled Betty in the beginning, and then realized that she had followed the wrong course and gave it up. Of course, the child resents the sudden loss of her high estate, and as the mother has probably overemphasized the importance of eating, Betty is attacking her weakest point. It is only in the rarest instances of severe organic disease of the brain that a child cannot swallow. Children, as well as adults who have difficulty in swallowing, usually want to attract attention at meal-time. They seem to be in great danger, make frantic efforts, and successfully frighten their table companions, but it is very difficult for anyone else to tell you how to swallow.

> "The worst meal is breakfast, at which Betty can hardly be forced to eat anything."

I am not sure whether I am correct in my explanation, but this appears to me like a child's morning song, as if Betty was giving her mother a hint of the difficulties she might expect during the day. Among many neurotics, especially in cases of melancholia, the symptoms are worse in the morning, as if the patients wanted to reiterate their sickness. Parents are much troubled if a child refuses to eat in the morning, probably because they believe that the child's health will suffer. It is easy to see how Betty's power grows and how she begins to rule the household by her refusal to eat. The child's goal seems to be that of domination over her family. To understand why she has chosen this goal, we must understand her position in the family. My first guess would be that she is an only child, and that, for some reason, it is vitally important to her to dominate her family.

> "For a long time she resorted to vomiting and had a number of food fads. If she was forced to eat she would vomit. Recently she had a fit of vomiting which was precipitated by an occurrence in school. The teacher insisted that she consume something which Betty had refused. Betty felt that this was an injustice, because she had called for double portions of everything else and had had a long record of eating at school and at home."

I have often insisted that children must not be forced to eat, because they are stronger than we are. I conclude from this report that Betty had a particularly strict teacher. The child's resistance met with harsh treatment, which was worse than the uncertain discipline at home. It used to be the usual procedure to throw cold water on a person or scream at her when she had a nervous fainting attack, and often this succeeded in stopping the attacks. But if improperly ambitious individuals fail to get their own way by means of such attacks, they simply look around for a more effective method. I remember the case of a very ambitious and domineering woman who could never bear to drive in traffic with her husband. When she was afraid and irritated she would grasp his hand or the wheel, to stop him or hinder him in driving. When she did this he would drive even faster, until she realized she could not restrain him. You may call this a cure or a treatment, but it reminds me of the curative measures which were common during the war. When a soldier developed hysteria and trembled, or could not speak, he was often tortured by the doctors by being shocked with an electric current. These soldiers would either stop their tremors or they would scream. This is not a treatment. Bodily symptoms which are based on psychological attitudes can be made to disappear very easily by using great force. But the individual's behavior pattern does not change thereby. He always finds another road to his fictitious rôle of superiority. It would be easy enough to stop Betty's food fads and vomiting, but at a later time she would develop other symptoms.

"There is a secondary problem, in that in the last two years she has evinced a growing unsocial attitude and increasing belligerency toward others, including her mother. She refuses to greet people."

We have already gathered that her attack was directed chiefly against the mother. The refusal to greet people is a very common symptom, and an interesting one to explain, because it is linked with the whole origin of greetings between individuals. Many children, whose goal is to dominate the grown-up environment, have difficulty in greeting their teachers or people on the street, because they feel that such a salutation is evidence of submission. In Vienna, for instance, this feeling of submission is not only implied but actually expressed. A common greeting is "Servus!" This actually means, "I am your slave." It is a form of salutation which goes back, I believe, to Roman times when a slave had to lift his hat to his master and say, "I am your slave." In America of course, the greeting is more an index of friendliness.

"Betty does not speak freely or civilly to people she meets and often uses abusive language. She will not forget a fancied wrong and goes from one fixed idea of grievance to another. At present she seems reluctant to experiment with the new; she shuns new situations and meeting new people, old or young, but she is ready to have someone else make the preliminary contacts when she happens to want to play with a strange child."

This is further evidence that the child's social interest has not developed.

> "She seems to think a great deal and often desires to be quiet for long periods of time, which she spends in brooding; but often she emerges from these moods with very intelligent questions."

Other schools of psychology, notably the school of Dr. Jung, in Zurich, would say that this contemplative attitude indicated that the child was an introvert. This child is an introvert, but it is not a congenital state, and we can understand how it has been artificially developed. Betty is isolated and unconnected with her companions, and therefore has nothing to do but to think. If the child liked companionship and had a strong social interest, Jung would call her an extrovert. This would simply mean that she had been properly educated and had grown up in a situation where she could experience and follow social interests. I do not believe that introversion and extroversion are fixed qualities.

> "The outdoors and nature are very dear to her. She asks constantly to live in the country, and when scenery is especially appealing she is moved to say with elation, 'Isn't the world beautiful?' "

When a child is social and still can be interested in nature it is very fortunate; but with this child who is not interested in human beings I am inclined to believe that she loves nature, not because of her courage, but because of her weakness. One often finds such a love of nature among people who are afraid to make social contacts, and would live wholly isolated from mankind on some little island, or in a hut in the forest.

> "The other day, however, when she seemed to be impressed with the freshness and beauty of the sunny morning she said pointedly, 'I like being cross.' "

This again indicates that she cannot make social connections, and that, therefore, being cross is one of the few spheres of activity which is left her. Being cross is also the best means to cross her mother, therefore, she likes it.

> "The parents say the eating problem has existed since she was born, but that her other difficulties are new developments."

This simply means that Betty has changed her instruments, but the general situation has not changed.

> "This immediate family consists of mother, father, and the one child. The relationship between the parents is a loving one, and the home may be said to be one of real marital happiness, although there is a considerable nervous tension due to economic stress and a long siege of illness in the mother's own family, with which she has

been in intimate contact. Both parents are high-strung, and outbursts of nerves have occurred from time to time."

An only child usually insists on being the center of attention, more than a child in a large family, and we have already considered how such a child, finding that the parents love each other dearly, feels discriminated against. When a marriage is unhappy, it is usually a problem for a child to adjust to, but we cannot insist that a happy marriage is the most important thing in bringing up children. We must always see the family situation in its relativity, before we can understand the relation of the child to its parents.

Now we have more clues concerning Betty's conflict with her mother. No doubt the mother's preoccupation with the illness in her family has detracted from her interest in her child. Outbursts of nerves on the part of parents are always difficult for children, especially if they are ambitious children, accustomed to holding the center of the stage. Such outbursts prevent Betty from having a chance to prove her superiority. She has been precluded by her lack of social interest from making contacts with people outside, and the nervous strain has closed the way for her within the family. The sole remaining sphere to express her superiority has been in the maintenance of her food fads.

"The father is a writer; the mother is at business. It is essential to have the combined incomes

> to make ends meet. The apartment contains four large bright rooms. The parents have a room to themselves. The child sleeps in her own bed, alone, although she shares her room with the maid. There is a paternal grandmother, who has been overanxious about the child's food and weight from the beginning, and constantly discusses these matters in the child's hearing. She has succeeded in imposing her fears on the parents."

A new complication. A grandmother usually overindulges children and makes it difficult for the mother, especially if she is a paternal grandmother. We hazard the guess that differences exist between the paternal grandmother and Betty's mother. The grandmother has increased the child's idea of the importance and significance of food and encouraged her to believe that eating is the most vital thing in the world.

> "The grandmother's attitude toward the mother has continued to be a critical one, even in the child's presence, and the mother believes that the grandmother's influence has precipitated the child's present critical and unfriendly attitude toward her."

It is natural for a child who wants to rule her family by being the center of attention, to take the side of a grandmother who is very kind and anxious and believes that the child is not fussed over enough. But the grandmother is probably not the entire cause of Betty's difficulties, though she has no doubt played an important rôle.

> "The child was in perfect health at birth, was breast-fed for seven months, and then weaned. Immediately thereafter, she was given impure milk, which caused a severe intestinal disorder that required a long time to heal. Her development was normal. She walked at the age of fourteen months and talked at fifteen months, speaking at once in sentences and forming plurals."

The intestinal disorder gives us another clue concerning the importance of eating in this family. The other data are important because they indicate that the child is unusually intelligent.

> "Her habits are excellent. She is quite cleanly but given to thumb-sucking. It was a tremendous task to break her of this habit."

Thumb-sucking is generally a means of attracting attention, and it was probably difficult to break Betty of the habit because she found this an easy way to assure herself of being constantly watched and guarded. However, there are some differing opinions about this habit. The Freudian interpretation of thumb-sucking is that it is a sexual complex and a perversion. A much more reasonable explanation is one which Dr. David M. Levy of the Institute of Child Guidance, in New York, has advocated. Dr. Levy found that if a child is breast-fed by a mother who has a great deal of milk which flows too readily, the proper exercise of the mouth and jaws is lacking and thumb-sucking is a compensation. While I believe Dr. Levy's explanation may be a factor in thumb-sucking, I also believe that any child can be made to form this habit if he feels that he is being watched and observed because of it.

> "When Betty's hands were bound she resorted to vomiting."

In other words, she proved herself the stronger in another way. Freud would say that she had to suppress her sex desire, and therefore vomited.

> "The mother cannot recall whether her first recourse to vomiting was a revolt against the restrictions or against the food. She has always been in violent revolt against prohibitions."

We can readily understand that children who want to dominate resent prohibitions. Such children cannot be influenced by punishment.

> "When less than two years old Betty replied when threatened with the loss of her toys: 'I don't care, I don't need them. I can look out of the window and think.'"

How easily this child maintains her fictional goal of superiority. It is the expression of her pride in being the stronger.

"The social position of the family is in the upper middle class. The parents' friends are chiefly professional people. The child submits more readily to her father and is very much attached to him. When the father caresses the mother, the child voices a definite protest such as 'Kiss me, too,' or 'I want a hug, too.' "

It is very evident that the child believes that the parents' affection for each other represents a subtraction from the love which is due her.

"It is necessary for the mother to work and at the age of two and one-half years the child was sent away for weeks with a well-trained, kindly nurse, in order to wean her from her mother, to whom she was devoted to a fault. The parents also hoped that by sending her away the feeding problem could be corrected. This was done shortly after the mother's enforced absence from home, due to family illness, during which time the child was inconsolable."

The sudden desertion of her indulgent mother was of course incomprehensible to Betty. It was a real tragedy for the child.

"While the child was away she grieved quietly for a few days, but was eventually won over to her situation and apparently became adjusted."

"Apparently" is the correct word to use, because later developments show that Betty never pardoned her mother.

> "The mother believes that the child never forgot the enforced absence, and never forgave it. Shortly after this she was sent to a private school of an experimental type."

The mother seems to have understood Betty's situation without knowing how to remedy it.

> "She revolted violently against the school, crying agonizingly, refusing to eat, and vomiting. This kept up for three months."

Betty shows a great deal of strength in carrying out her protest. In a way I consider this a promising sign, because if this strength can be directed into useful channels the child will become a leader.

> "Then the child suddenly announced that she would go to school without crying, and since then there has been no trouble on this score. She is now in her third year kindergarten, and is quite popular."

The reason for her sudden change must have been that she either found a better way to master her problems at school or a more advantageous situation. Her popularity is rather surprising in view of her lack of interest in other children. However, many spoiled children are able to develop a splendid technique for attracting people; this has probably happened in Betty's case.

> "Until recently she had a very marked attraction for older boys, and used her charm with relish. Her influence was so unusual that the teachers made efforts to learn how she managed to win the boys, but they could not learn her procedure."

This is confirmation of our belief that she has a good technique for getting other people to pamper her. Her procedure with the boys was probably the same that she used to conciliate her father.

> "She was away at a summer camp run by one of the teachers of her school, for the past two summers, remaining away from home three months each time. Last year this was supplemented by a two weeks' trip with another child and that child's parents. She conducted herself so graciously that the parents were loud in her praise. Each year, however, she announces in advance that she will not go away, and she is quite insistent this year as well, but each year she goes quite gladly."

Here we have more evidence that the child knows how to endear herself to people. As far as her protests against going away are concerned, she uses these merely as a means to trouble her parents.

"This year she insists on going away with her mother as her school friends do."

Now this is the fire that burns in her soul: she wants to be with her mother. She very intelligently takes her mother to task: "My friends go with their mothers, and I want to go with you."

"Her recreations are normal. She has no street friends, for she is at school until half past four every afternoon. Her inclinations are toward the piano, at which she has decided talent, and although she has not yet been tutored she has composed some very beautiful little pieces. Her teacher in school says she does everything well when she tries. It is being noticed that she is sensitive about her work. She is not at ease unless she thinks she excels and refuses to work or play when she fears that she will not show to advantage."

Betty's conduct is irreproachable in school, because any reproof would be too grave an insult to her pride and ambition.

"She feels the absence of a sister or brother and complains that she has no one to play with at home. Friends are called in, but there is always trouble when she is left alone again and there is a constant and intense protest about the mother's work and absence from home."

It is doubtful whether she really wants a brother or sister, and probably she is certain that she will not have either one. Her complaints are to be considered rather as an accusation against her mother. She really wants her mother to be at home, occupied solely with her.

> "The child has tried by tears, prayers, and incriminations, to keep the mother at home. She says for example, 'I'll be your friend if you will only stay at home.' The day's routine is normal for her age. She sleeps well, so far as it is known, without dreaming, with the exception of a few occasions when she awoke screaming, saying that lions and tigers were coming up the stairs."

Betty has finally found a way to irritate and occupy her parents at night. Lions and tigers are very useful for this purpose.

> "The mother takes her to school every morning, and the father frequently calls for her. Since infancy this child's interest, almost to the exclusion of everything else, seems to have been in watching the reactions of people, both children and adults. This tendency is so marked that she will at times provoke a reaction simply to observe and comment upon it. She is very quick to report accurately the idiosyncrasies of those whom she watches. Her mind is decidedly logical and analytical."

What does this mean? It is an obvious imitation of the father, who, as a writer, must constantly observe the reactions of people. Many of you no doubt know the superstition that women cannot be logical and analytical, but here is an example that proves its fallacy. Any girl can be logical and analytical when, as is the case here, it serves her purpose.

> "She invented the following game. Betty was a judge while her playmates took the rôles of policemen, who had arrested a naked woman and arraigned her before Judge Betty. Then Judge Betty pronounced the following sentence: 'The only thing to do with a naked woman is to electrocute her.' "

This is a significant game, because it shows in the first place that she has understood the difference between the sexes, and in the second that she has developed the feeling of inferiority; she does not speak of naked men but of naked women. It is her masculine protest. An index at one and the same time that she resents being a woman and that she wants to be a man. We need not be surprised that she imitates her father. Her high ambition is not consistent with her idea of the feminine rôle.

> "Nudity as such is not a startling fact to her, as she has constantly seen her campmates naked and her parents are quite casual about her seeing

> them bathe, should she happen to come to the bathroom."

The object of Betty's intolerance is not nudity, but women.

> "For a long time she demanded to be told stories about bad animals and bad people. The good stories do not interest her."

Very likely the stories about bad animals are useful material with which to trouble her mother at night. Individuals who have no social interest like to believe that people are naturally bad. Most egoistic philosophers have sponsored such theories. Socially interested individuals are usually tolerant and kind and try to understand the factors which make people bad. Moreover, stories of good people are really not very interesting to read. Nobody would be interested in the story of a good man who always got up smiling in the morning, said kind words to his family, went to work with a laugh, brought home presents to his children and flowers to his wife, and was always kind, sweet, and gentle. But if you tell a story of a bad man who is cruel and thoughtless, you can get people to read it.

> "Recently in a very dramatic fashion, the girl threatened her schoolmates as follows: 'If you don't do such and such, I'll send the influenza to get you tonight, I'll send it through the open window and you'll die.' Finally she believed the story herself and insisted on the window's being shut."

You see her striving for magic power in the phrase, "You will die." She is beginning to assume the rôle of godlikeness. She wants to be master of life and death, to make people die when they do not obey her. Herein lies the tragedy of such a child's life. The lack of social interest and her dominating attitude will be revenged upon her own person. Whoso uses this sword will perish by it. This is the cruel logic of life.

I have been told that the child is sick this evening, so that we can speak only with the mother. I am not sure whether we can persuade her to our point of view, but it will be our problem to explain the situation to her, and she will have to explain it to Betty. In many ways the mother has acted very correctly, and has understood the coherence of her child's behavior. She will have to explain to Betty that eating is not the vital matter that the grandmother thinks it, but in such a way that the grandmother will not be hurt. The child can be told, for instance, that the grandmother means well, but is not sufficiently versed in these matters. The child should have more friends, and be encouraged to train herself toward a useful leadership among them.

### Conference

The mother comes in.

Dr. Adler. We have carefully considered the story of your little girl and find that she is a very intelligent and promising child. I think that your understanding of her conduct has been excellent in many respects. It seems to me that the child felt that she was deserted when you were busy with your family and has not forgiven you for it. She does not realize that her life's purpose now is to punish you for this desertion, but I believe that if you speak with her about it you can convince her of your friendship.

MOTHER. I have done that time and time again, but she is not interested. She is very abstract about the matter, and so emotionally involved and so resentful that she will not allow her mental faculties to operate. She is very irritated about my position, and says, "Why don't you get a position with my school?" I tell her there is no position for me in her school, and in the second place, I could not earn enough money that way.

DR. ADLER. I would suggest that you tell her you will try it for fourteen days to see how she will like going hungry because you are not earning sufficient money. I doubt whether she will consent to this, because I see the matter of eating is very much exaggerated in your family.

MOTHER. That's true.

Mother tells about the influenza and about the child's watching other human beings.

DR. ADLER. Her terror of the influenza is to show you that she really has the power to call down the influenza on her playmates. You might explain it to her in this way. Tell her also that since babyhood she has wanted to be the center of attention.

MOTHER. I have tried to rationalize her and have progressed to a certain extent, but then I have been blocked.

DR. ADLER. You probably did not find the right catchword. Take a walk with her and in a friendly way tell her that to have been forced to leave her hurt you very much. Impress upon her that you would prefer being with her as much as possible, and then appeal to her reason and ask her if she would not also work if she had to take care of a family. Then remind her that she is an only child and suggest that she is trying to rule the family by making difficulties about her eating. You might say to her that you are not entirely certain whether this is so, and you would like to discuss it with her.

MOTHER. Recently there have been several deaths in the family due to tuberculosis and other causes. Since these deaths she has been very bad about eating. She is quite conscious of what she does. She says, "If I don't eat tonight, I am sure I shall not die."

DR. ADLER. She only wants to irritate you and occupy you with her interests. What she really means is, "I will not eat. Are you not afraid that I shall die?" Then she believes you will be worried and force her to eat.

MOTHER. She is really not so disturbing about her eating as she is about her other reactions. She is not at all interested in her associates.

DR. ADLER. I believe this can best be settled in

school. Her teacher will talk to her as a real friend and show her how she can be the leader of other children, not by ruling them and attacking them, but by helping them. You may discuss this point with her too if you like, but do not criticize her. I believe you understand what I mean. Her goal in life is to irritate you, which is common among only children, especially if they have been overindulged once, and then been deserted. We must make her more sociable and more interested in other people, and you can do this best by dropping a friendly hint here and there as to how it can be done. The child is very contemplative and will understand it. Is she not sure that she will always be an only child?

MOTHER. Yes.

DR. ADLER. You see how clever she is. She knows that she can pray for another child, and that her prayer will not be granted. Have you noticed that she would prefer to be a boy?

MOTHER. Yes, she believes that boys have more freedom.

DR. ADLER. She feels inferior, so she fights and is abusive. Nevertheless, I am sure that she is a fine girl. If she is abusive, then you can tell her that swearing is not especially clever and that really fine adults never do it. You must be more free with her and take her into your confidence, ask her opinion about little matters in the household, treat her as a grown-up and let her feel that she can win significance by assuming responsibilities and by being kind. You must also explain to her that she has always tried to dominate the family and point out that neither you nor your husband try to dominate; that the family is a partnership, one for all, and all for one.

MOTHER. I think that is a very good idea.

## *FOLLOW THE LEADER*

THIS evening we have under consideration the case history of Michael, a boy twelve years and eight months old, who has been caught in a number of robberies. He is a member of a roughly organized gang, led by a boy of fourteen years, who teaches these younger boys how to steal.

Our first impression is that Michael must be seriously dissatisfied with the conditions of his environment. If the leader of the gang influences him to steal it is evident that he has more significance among these boys than in school or at home. The notes state:

> "He has been stealing for quite some time, until 'Baldy,' who was the leader, was sent away to a home. This was about two years ago. Now Baldy is back in the neighborhood, and the boys have been caught in several robberies."

An important factor is that the boy does not steal independently. He is used and abused by the gang. Perhaps the leader flatters Michael's egotism, or perhaps Michael is one of those feeble-minded, or almost feeble-minded, children who are blindly obedient to their accepted chief. Anyone who has studied criminal cases knows that members of this type are to be found in every gang. They are the cat's-paws who do the actual stealing. It is probable that this child is not feeble-minded, but he is certainly extremely dependent on others. He wants to be an underling, and acquires a distorted sense of superiority in blindly following his leader's commands.

> "Michael was taken to the Children's Court and is now on probation."

It is hardly in order to discuss here whether probation for children is a good thing or not. But for a child only twelve years old to be on probation to the court is an important difficulty which may add to his feeling of degradation and humiliation.

> "The father and mother were born in Ukrainia and the mother speaks very little English. The father speaks English fairly well. They have lived in New York about three years. The father works from eight to five in a factory, the mother works from five to nine cleaning offices. Both parents are naturalized citizens, and the children were all born in America."

The mother's inability to speak English readily is an additional handicap. Such little things can easily hinder a child's social development. Furthermore, when the children are at home the parents are practically never there together.

> "There are three children, Leon, aged fourteen years and six months, Michael, aged twelve years and eight months, and Mary, aged six. They live in a four-room flat of the old tenement type. There are no elevators, no bath, no heat, and the toilet is in the hall. There are two bedrooms. Michael and Leon sleep together. The family is Catholic."

It is probable that Michael's older brother has developed the characteristics of a leader, and that Michael has submitted to him in order to feel his equal, as his companion and partner. By allowing himself to be led he gains the leader's attention and appreciation. His brother is two years older, and his sister is six years younger, so the older brother probably influenced his pattern more than the younger sister. The description of the home shows that they are very poor, and the family situation may be bad.

> "Michael had a normal birth and development. He walked at one year, and talked soon after that. He seems affectionate and friendly with everyone, including his own family. At school he is popular and gets on well with the other children."

The history confirms our assumptions about this child's psychology. He is friendly and submissive and therefore unlikely to be the leader in any misdemeanor.

> "Michael says he had some teachers that he did not like, but he likes his present teacher."

Obviously he wants to be treated kindly, and his conduct is in the nature of a pact with authority, "Be good to me and I will be good to you." It is because he is so humble that he can be led into crime. It would be just as easy to lead him to do good things, but this would be insufficient. He must also be taught to be independent and self-confident. It is not enough to admonish him and preach to him. He must be given a sense of his own responsibility.

> "He plays on the street much of the time. He plays tag, and ball games, and shoots dice, is generally well liked by other children and easily led by bigger boys."

Our presuppositions are being confirmed over and over again by the case history. Michael will do anything to be appreciated.

> "Michael says he has a girl whom he takes to the movies sometimes and whose house he sometimes visits. He and his brother take turns in shining shoes. They have a bootblack outfit and go out after school and on Saturdays."

"He and his brother." Again the confirmation of the fact that he must be with a leader. Going out with girls is a patent gesture of imitation of the older boys.

"Michael's mother says, 'Mike a good boy. He always happy at home. Loves to play with his young sister, teases her sometimes. I do not know he is going with Baldy. Baldy very bad boy. Mike never get in trouble until he meet with Baldy. He stayed away from school two times, once when he went to Coney Island, once when I wanted him to go to hospital with me. I not speak so good. Mike now going with bad boys. I think we try to move, so Mike go with better boys.'

"The mother says that when she goes to work at five o'clock the father looks after Michael and does not let him run out. She wants him to go to the Settlement House every afternoon, so that he will not go out on the street. Michael often earns one or two dollars which he takes home to his mother and she gives him a nickel or a dime."

Although it is good for a boy to contribute his earnings to the family, perhaps in this case it is a further indication of self-abasement. The mother is quite right about moving into a different neighborhood. It is better to move such a child, if he is being constantly tempted, than to expose him to a vicious situation. Michael can be led by his father, but as the father cannot always be at home, Michael comes under the influence of older boys. The only real cure is to make him more independent.

"The father says, 'Mike is not bad. He never takes money at home, although he could take it from my pocketbook.' Leon takes the older-brother attitude toward Mike. He will fight for him and with him. The older brother eagerly tells how he beat up another boy in his brother's defense, but he feels very much superior to Michael. He is farther along in school and gets better marks. He does not steal or play dice."

The case history continues to confirm our earlier conjectures. The older brother fights with Michael and suppresses him in order to overcome his own innate feeling of inferiority, while Michael worships his brother as a hero.

"Michael says, 'My father and mother like Leon best.' Leon eagerly confirms this and adds that his little sister likes him best too. Michael is very fond of his mother and his little sister, and does not show resentment of the family disapproval, although I know he feels it."

His lack of resentment probably means that Michael tolerates his subordinate position only to derive certain advantages from it. It is important to know whether the child's mentality is really of a low order, and for this information we must go to the school report.

"Michael was born in a factory town in New York, and both mother and father worked all day in the factory. The children were taken to a nursery at eight in the morning, and called for at five or six in the evening. This lasted for three years. Then the children were sent to a Catholic school. When Michael was eight years old the family moved to Michigan, but returned to New York the same year. This change cost Michael a year in school. Although he was past eight years, he was put in the first grade. He is now in the 4A junior shop. His best marks are in arithmetic, his poorest in reading and spelling."

It is probable that he was humiliated by this loss of a year, which put him in a class with younger boys. He may be a left-handed child, for his nickname is Lefty.

"The teacher says: 'I like Michael, and the children like him. He does not quarrel. The intelligence test shows that he has an intelligence quotient of 70. A motor-mechanical showed that he had good ability in using his hands, his score being average for his age. An emotional test indicated that he is much concerned over the robberies and with being taken to the Children's Court. He appears to be afraid of the older boys in the gang.' "

The low I.Q. would lead many people to believe that this child was feeble-minded, but it must be remembered that his life pattern is one of discouragement and fear. I am very much in favor of removing him to a more favorable situation.

"Last summer Michael went to a free camp for two months. His record was best in swimming, good in athletics and music. His attitude was co-operative and helpful. The counselor remarked: 'Mike was one of the bright spots of the season. He possesses the cheeriest smile I have ever seen and it was always in evidence. He is a typical happy-go-lucky type. His routine work and play were always done in a spirit of gaiety.'"

Michael would be quite ready to destroy himself if someone asked him to do so, as a favor. The counselor, beset by many problem boys, would of course appreciate a child who was a good athlete and always cheerful. He smiles so constantly because he puts all responsibility for his actions in other people's hands. This child would never be a problem in a favorable environment.

"For several months previous to March 30, 1929, the boy had committed a number of petty thefts, which culminated in a good-sized robbery of several pocketbooks, the contents of which amounted to $60. They were taken to an open room where a class was in progress. The theft was traced to the gang of which Baldy was the leader, another boy the brains, and Michael the tool."

It has been perfectly clear that Michael would not be the instigator or leader in an activity of this kind.

"In Michael's confession he said that he came in the front hall and got the elevator man, who has charge of the building, to chase him. He said the elevator man threatened to wring his neck if he caught him. While he was being chased, the other boys climbed into the building and stole the pocketbooks and watches, and divided the money."

To be chased by an elevator man is not exactly an heroic rôle.

"In the Brooklyn robbery, Michael said that he did not take anything. He said his job was to 'watch for the cops.' When he saw one coming he called, 'Chicki,' and the other boys ran. Incidentally not fast enough, for they were all caught and taken to court."

Again he plays an inferior part.

"This gang also shoots crap on Sundays in front of Michael's house. Michael is afraid of Baldy. 'Baldy bites when he fights.' "

His subservience, in this instance, is probably based on fear alone.

"His earliest recollection is, 'I remember when we lived in Little Falls, we used to steal watermelons.' "

It is interesting that he does not say, "*I* used to steal." Michael is never solitary. I doubt if he understands that it is wrong to steal. He is more or less hypnotized by the gang spirit, for in the gang he loses his personal identity and responsibility.

> " 'I remember when I was little there was a rat hole in the floor and I was putting matches in it and a match fell on the bed and it caught fire. My brother ran down-stairs and got my father.' "

This recollection shows Michael's conviction that when he attempts any independent activity, failure and catastrophe are sure to follow. He is equally certain that there will always be someone to help him. This is a child who has never overcome his original feeling of inferiority and is desperately afraid to venture anything on his own responsibility. His life has been a succession of scenes in which he has been completely dominated by his brother, by his teacher, by Baldy, and by his gang companions.

> " 'I dreamed that I was in a palace, a castle, with big rooms that were very nice.' "

Perhaps this is evidence of Michael's desire for a more important position in life.

> "Another dream: 'When I was sleeping one night, a man came in and robbed my mother and shot my brother. I got on a horse and chased him and shot him twice in the heart and threw him off his horse.

"'I dreamed that my mother died, and I was crying and I wanted to get the guy that killed my mother and I got him and killed him. He was a big gangster.'"

In this dream he plays the rôle of a hero. It also shows his fear of losing any of his family. Emotionally the dream says, "I am glad that I have my mother and brother, because I am so weak." He can imagine no greater calamity than to be left without a leader.

"To the question, 'What would you like to be when you grow up?' Michael instantly replied, 'Police commissioner.'"

Michael wants to be a police commissioner, because his ideal symbolizes the commander, the strongest man. It is a compensation for his own weakness.

The teacher's interpretation of the case is as follows:

"Michael has really not had a fair chance, because his mother has had to work most of the time. His brother Leon makes a much better showing both at school and at home. His younger sister took his place when he was six years old, and now, although he loves her very much, she prefers Leon to him. Michael's schooling has been another cause for discouragement. When he had a chance to join the gang, which no doubt received him gladly, he did so. The treatment that is advised, is that he be recommended to return to camp where he was last summer. This will put him in a good environment for two months and give him a chance to do the things in which he excels, such as swimming. We have advised that Michael and Leon be placed under different counselors, so that Michael can gain strength and courage in his own right. We are trying to have the family see Michael, not as a disgrace, but as an asset."

This is a good way to start, but it is only a beginning. Michael must understand why he insists on playing an inferior rôle. He should be encouraged to believe that he is capable of being his own leader. In talking to Michael, it will be better not to speak of the robberies. We need concern ourselves only with his undervaluation of himself. We must find out whether he is really a left-handed child, and whether he needs special training in reading and spelling.

### Conference

The father comes in.

Dr. Adler. We should like to speak to you about your son, Michael, whom we find a very promising boy. His greatest mistake is that he likes to be led too much. His whole personality is built upon this mistake, and for this reason he is not very courageous and wants someone else to take the responsibility for his actions. Have you noticed that he is not brave, that he is afraid of the dark, that he does not like to be left alone?

FATHER. Yes, I know that he does not like to be left alone.

DR. ADLER. You can do a great deal to help him. He should not be punished. He is not really guilty. He must be encouraged and convinced that he is strong enough to accomplish everything by himself without the help of his brother and his gang. I believe that he is a good boy, and it is only necessary to show him where he has made his mistake. Do not reproach him or punish him, but encourage him to be stronger, and he will be more responsible.

The boy comes in.

DR. ADLER. Why, you are a great, strong boy! I thought you were little and weak, and it's not so at all. Why do you believe that other boys know more and understand more than you do, and that you must listen to what they say and do what they ask you to do? Would you climb this wall if somebody told you to?

MICHAEL. Yes.

DR. ADLER. You are an intelligent boy and do not need a leader. You are big enough to be independent and courageous and be a leader yourself. You can get rid of the idea that other people do things better than you do. Do you think you must always be a slave to other boys and do what they command? How long would it take you to stop doing everything they tell you? Do you think you can do it in four days?

MICHAEL. Maybe.

DR. ADLER. Eight days?

MICHAEL. Yes, I can do it in eight days.

Michael goes out.

DR. ADLER. We have no rules, but our task in this case is obviously to bring Michael to the useful side of life by changing his pattern to a more courageous one. His ambition was too hard for him to attain, and so he satisfies himself with what he can get.

STUDENT. Is his constant smile a sign that he is trying to win others over to take care of him?

DR. ADLER. Yes, very likely that is one reason.

STUDENT. How can you make him feel that it is worth while to be courageous?

DR. ADLER. Courage cannot be given like a spoonful of medicine. What we must do is to show him that he will be happier if he does not undervalue himself, and he will discover the advantages of courage as soon as we can get him to resist the commands of his gang. I tried to show him that it is a mistake to be always led. If we add to his self-esteem, courage will come of itself. So long as he feels inferior he will not accept responsibility. The training to be responsible and the training to be courageous are all part of the same thing.

STUDENT. Were you not a little more severe with this boy than with the others?

Dr. Adler. I must confess that, if so, it was not intentional, but I hope that I spoke to him as wisely as possible. The art of speaking to a child must be learned and it is quite possible that I, as well as others, make mistakes. No two people will approach a child in the same way. Personally, I like a rather dramatic manner, because this helps the child to identify himself as an important actor in the conversation. I tried to be very friendly with the child, and I should not be surprised if he likes me and would be willing to come here again. Perhaps the teacher will give us a report on his further progress.

## *THE TOO DOCILE CHILD*

THIS evening we have the case of Saul, who is eight and one-half years old. The present problem is that he does not get along well at school, a situation of long standing.

With an eight-and-one-half-year-old child who cannot get along in school, there are always two possibilities to consider. The child is either feeble-minded or he is unable to adjust himself to school conditions because he has been used to a more favorable situation in the home.

The case notes state:

> "In the last two or three weeks there seems to be an improvement, owing to the fact that the person in charge of the school, who is attending these lectures on Individual Psychology, seems to have gained a better insight into his problem."

Apparently we have the second of the two possibilities here, and I am very happy to learn that these lectures have been a practical benefit.

> "Saul seems quite indifferent to his standing in school and says he does not know how to do his work. After considerable pressure on the child in

> private conference, it was found that he did possess some knowledge, although it was difficult to determine the extent of his understanding, because he made no effort at all to produce any facts from his memory."

If a child has given up hope, and believes progress is impossible, his attitude is best expressed by a lack of memory and an ignorance of facts.

> "He would not do his arithmetic, yet he had some knowledge of processes and combinations. He would scrawl on a paper or leave it blank, except at fitful intervals. His conduct was very poor and interfered decidedly with school work. He would leave his seat and wander around, attack other children for real or fancied slights, talk aloud and especially attempt to be funny and make children laugh by gestures, ways of walking, and joking. He seemed to have a certain amount of dramatic power and would have been funny had he done the same things at the right time. But there is no place in school for this kind of action, and he was what the long-suffering teachers called 'an impossible child,' which very well describes his relation to the classroom."

Saul plays the rôle of a clown in order to be the center of attention. He uses the cheap means at his disposal because he does not trust himself to gain the limelight of the classroom in a useful way.

> "He cries easily . . ."

This makes me think he has been petted until he has come to believe himself such a valuable person that if he suffers, others must suffer also.

> ". . . and seems rather babyish when reproved. This conduct alternates with his attempts to be funny."

A spoiled child very often likes to play the rôle of a baby. He uses two means to gain attention—either he is a comedian or a baby.

> "He quarreled and fought with school children older than himself. He was always in trouble at recess or when coming and going to school."

This sort of behavior shows that he is not socially adjusted.

> "Sometimes he tells fantastic stories. He was promoted from the last class, and the chances are that he would have improved, but he told the new teacher that he was promoted because his father and the father of the former teacher were friends. (They were friends, but the teacher was not the one who decided his promotion.)"

The fact that he accuses the teacher of fraud indicates that he is not at all willing to cooperate.

> "One day as an excuse for not doing his home work he told the teacher that his house had

burned down. (There had been a fire in his aunt's house.)"

He is beginning to lie to save himself from difficult situations.

> "His stories were evidently suggested by facts which he deliberately injected into his own life, but at the time they were told no one knew that they were derived from veritable occurrences. Saul knew he was not telling the truth and admitted it under pressure. His past problems were similar. He had no trouble in the kindergarten where no scholastic results were required of him, but as soon as he entered the grade, at the age of six, the trouble began and has increased with each grade."

The less you demand of such a child, the less trouble you will have. In the comparatively easy situation of the kindergarten, he gave no trouble, but when he was confronted with mature tasks, the boy began to protest. He had not learned to work independently. If we review our knowledge of the case, up to this point, our conclusion must be that he is a spoiled child who has made progressive resistance to the problems of growing up. The nearer he approaches these problems the harder he protests, trying to evade the issues and escape to the useless side of life.

Formerly his life ran along very quietly, and he gave no trouble until he entered school. If we have been given all the necessary facts, and nothing is omitted from the case history, we may be reasonably sure that his mother spoiled him, and still does.

> "The parents are living. There are two children, Saul, eight and one-half, and Sarah, who is five years old."

Here again we have the problem of an older boy and a younger sister. There must be considerable competition between these two children, and I imagine, if we investigate thoroughly, we shall find that the trouble began when he was three or four years old and was forced to face the rivalry of his sister. It is probable that he began losing his courage and self-confidence at this time and began to insist by his actions that he wanted his mother's overindulgence to continue. Probably his sister is a strong, healthy child whose progress is making inroads into his domain.

> "The relation between the parents is excellent; the mother, though quiet in manner, rules; the father works for a moving-van concern and gets a small salary, which varies somewhat each week. The mother is economical and an excellent housekeeper. She does all the laundry work herself, but tells her neighbors she sends it to the laundry, because these neighbors send out their laundry and she wants to keep up appearances. The father brings his wages home each week and is proud of her excellent management and neat home."

These facts show us that the mother is proud and ambitious, and that her husband is also leaning on her.

> "The mother keeps both children up to the mark in every way as to neatness, obedience, good health habits, and the like. She supervises where, and with whom the children play. She is an excellent wife and mother. The father is more impulsive and has great faith in his wife and is kind to the children. He cannot manage Saul as well as the mother can, and on this account the mother thinks Saul prefers his father. Saul is helpful, likes to assist with housework, go on errands for his mother and take care of the room which he shares with his little sister."

Our patient has no resistance to his sister because he is with her too much. I believe if he spent more time with his father he would be more critical of her.

> "Each child has a separate bed. When the mother was ill, Saul showed great solicitude about her, running down to the drug store of his own accord to get help."

These again are signs that the child depends on his mother, and it is probable that he wishes to appear a hero in her eyes.

> "When his mother punishes him he cries a little but quickly gets over it. He shows no resent-

ment, but says, 'All right, you're the boss; you're the mother, you're right.' His mother does not praise him overmuch, but in the last two or three weeks he has been praised for his improvement in school."

The boy's attitude toward punishment is the humble criticism of a weak person, but I think he will get more courage as his school work shows improvement.

"The little sister is very attractive, and though not spoiled, the whole family pet her. Saul is very fond of her."

This would seem to upset our interpretation, were it not for the fact that Saul probably recognizes that he has been conquered by the enemy, and as he has lost hope of winning the battle he makes friends with his conqueror. It is not unusual for dethroned children to express fondness for those who have displaced them.

"He is afraid that the gipsies will kidnap her in the street."

By this attitude he makes capital of his sense of being dominated.

"His mother gives him six cents, he spends five for milk and often gives the penny to his little sister. Mother says Saul is like his father —generous. Sister takes this as a matter of course. When the boys on the street want to tease him, she tells them not to. He gets a good deal of teasing in the street."

Saul plays the rôle of protector, which is a good way to reconcile an older brother to a sister, because it gives him an opportunity to feel grown up. On the other hand, the sister also wants to protect her brother.

"He plays chiefly with boys who are related to him. They call him "Fat" because he is very fat; they also call him a "dope" because of his school difficulties. When his uncles also called him stupid, his mother requested them not to."

The most common reason for excess of fat is overeating. But, on the other hand, he may have some glandular illness which causes obesity. The mother is right when she cautions the uncles not to humiliate him.

"He fights and, though he gets the worst of it, he generally fights on."

It is not unusual to find that hopeless children fight with the conviction that they will be beaten.

"He is exceedingly kind to animals and likes flowers."

This type of boy ordinarily prefers a quiet life, and probably if Saul were not teased or attacked he would be interested in the care of animals and plants.

"He goes to the movies and they fill a great deal of his thoughts."

I ought to say a word here about the movies. I doubt very much whether they can be wholly responsible for incorrect development in a child, but I am certain that if mistakes have been made in the home, moving pictures may intensify them, and the child may obtain data for his mistaken pattern. We can hardly expect to change his pattern by forbidding the movies, because he would find another way to train himself. In Europe there is a strict censorship which decides whether children can see a moving picture or not, but this is surely not enough, for we cannot prevent adults, often the parents of children, from training themselves for a false pattern. The movies accustom people to cunning and slyness. Most movies depend for their appeal upon tricks, and that is what children and adults want to learn—a quick way to power. Many people believe that craftiness and trickery are advantageous, but we can hardly agree with this from the psychological point of view. To us the use of such methods is only a sign that an individual is not courageous, and we should educate people to this realization. Tricks, slyness, and cunning should be recognized as the devices of a coward. We may laugh at them and be astonished by their efficacy, but in our deeper conscience we ought to know that they are used only by people who do not trust their own powers toward a normal goal.

"The child was healthy when born, but the delivery had to be made with instruments. He was breast-fed for nine months and then fed on the bottle. Talked at one year, walked at fifteen months; between the ages of eighteen months and two years, he had convulsions at four different times. After the teeth came, there were no more convulsions."

It is fairly certain that this child had some difficulty with his parathyroid gland. The convulsions had nothing whatsoever to do with the eruption of the teeth.

"He had measles at two years, and chicken pox at four. At present he eats well, is healthy, but is not greedy."

If the child were greedy it would show a certain degree of stubbornness. This boy is evidently not of the resistant type, but is much more inclined to submit.

"He is very neat in his habits and has never had enuresis."

We might well have expected this child to have had enuresis and difficulties in eating, but his mother has apparently managed him with considerable understanding. I am sure that when we speak with her we shall have the impression that she is an intelligent woman.

> "He likes to look neat and demands a clean blouse for school each day. He likes his mother to wash and dress him, but he is independent in his sleeping. As a baby he was wakeful and required a great deal of rocking, but he sleeps well now."

He imitates his mother in being neat because this gains her attention. Her technique of treating his sleeping difficulties seems to have improved with time.

> "He collects small pictures and postal cards."

In other words, he feels that he must add to his diminished prestige by the accumulation of objects. This boy is likely to steal if his situation is not improved.

> "He may need glasses and is being examined this week to ascertain whether a visual defect exists."

There may be some difficulty in persuading Saul to wear glasses.

> "His earliest recollection is that he visited his grandmother when he was three years old, and was punished by his mother for enuresis. His mother says this was not a usual habit with him."

This must have been one of the first times when he felt his importance threatened, and he tried to gain the attention of his mother by wetting his bed, only to find that he was punished instead.

"Another recollection dates from the age of four. He was with his father in a moving van and when his father was not looking, he helped move a number of small objects out of the van, evidently with great satisfaction."

This shows a helpful attitude and perhaps his remembering the episode signifies a desire to win his father's approbation.

"He remembers when his sister was born when he was three and one-half years old. He says his mother gave him candy at that time."

The birth of his sister presented a real problem, and I doubt if the candy reconciled him to her presence.

"There are a number of dreams which he remembers. (Dream 1) 'I dreamed I was with a cowboy and I was on a horse; the horse turned into a nanny-goat; I had the cowboy's gun. When I shot once, the gun went off, but the second time it was a trick gun and it didn't go off.' "

We see the emphasis on tricks in this dream. A horse changes into a nanny-goat, a trick gun fails to go off. This boy is looking for tricks to change himself.

"(Dream 2) 'I dreamed I was on a horse and I was Rudolph Valentino. When a man dies I dream about him.' "

It is obvious that he is molding himself on moving picture heroes.

> " 'I dreamed about William S. Hart. I dreamed he kidnaped me and ran away with me.' "

Here is one of the dangers of moving pictures. Kidnaping plays entirely too important a rôle in his life. About the death dream. If he dreams about men after they die, he is trying to avoid death. But if he says he dreams about them before they died, it would indicate an effort to be a prophet.

> "It is his ambition to be a movie actor. He is deeply interested in them all, and his hero is Tom Mix."

This ambition is not surprising in view of the fact that he has been playing a rôle all during his school life. The rôle of a clown, of a comedian, of an actor interested in tricks. He wants to overcome dangers, to be powerful, and probably he believes that being a moving picture actor is a way to attain his ends.

> "The following conversation shows his fears. *Saul:* I am afraid of Rudolph Valentino—I see him in my sleep. *Q.* Don't you know he is dead? *Saul:* Yes, I know. I know why he died. He was too nice; all the women liked him."

Remember that this is a boy of eight and one-half years. It is amazing how early the fear of love and women may be definitely part of a child's pattern. It is not hard to understand why Saul has this attitude. He has a very strong mother, and I have already spoken of the fact that boys with masterful mothers are frequently afraid of women. Later in life, when this fear or exclusion of women becomes fixed, the individual may become a homosexual. Here we have the process in the making, and in order to prevent it we must influence the mother not to dominate her son too much.

> "*Saul.* One day a woman put poison in his food; she put in a little every day until he died. My father showed me the picture. When his wife woke up, she didn't find him any more. *Q.* Did his wife do this? *Saul.* No, a different lady."

Here again we have the influence of movie training.

> "Teacher's discussion of the case: 'About three weeks ago, I judged that Saul's attempts to be an entertaining actor in the classroom agreed with the description of a discouraged child, blocked on all sides. Therefore I gave him more praise than his work deserved and excessive encouragement. He is beginning to respond; his eyes have lost their dull expression, and he shows some ambition. He is taking home good reports and he is promising his mother to do better yet. It seems that he is a courageous child, for he explained to me that one day his mother dropped a clothes-pin

into the yard in the dark and he went down-stairs to get it, without fear.' "

He wants to be a hero when his mother is looking on.

" 'His fighting would show his courage. He is not timid and does not pretend to be. His pretense is that he does not know his work. There may be a certain amount of handicap from his eyes, but it will be corrected this week if it exists. His objections to the names the boys call him can be removed if he learns to take them good-naturedly. He has been told that boys often nickname each other, that there is a colored boy, for instance, in his class who has been nicknamed Farina, and likes it.' "

About nicknames. It is true that if a boy has other advantages, nicknames do not trouble him much.

I see that Saul's teacher has found the best way to influence him and I am sure that she will be successful. Her success will be more stable if the boy's mother ceases to dominate him and if he is assured that he has every chance to progress and that the fear of his sister's overtaking him is groundless. He must realize that girls develop more quickly than boys and that he in turn will later develop more quickly than his sister. His mother should be persuaded to take him more seriously. It is not wise to make this boy too obedient. Let her discuss her plans with him, and never demand anything from him, simply because she wants it. She should take him into her confidence, explain things to him in greater detail, and even seek his advice. "Would it not be better if you washed and dressed alone?" "Do you not think this would be good for your sister?"

## Conference

The mother enters, accompanied by the teacher who is presenting the case, and is introduced to Dr. Adler.

Dr. Adler. In many ways you have been very sensible in dealing with your son. You have guided him from certain dangers which children frequently cannot surmount.

Mother. I have tried to make him a good boy.

Dr. Adler. He is a good boy but he finds things very difficult in school. Probably the origin of his difficulties is the fact that he was an only child for three and one-half years and found life easier than he does today. He is not a coward and he has not made the mistakes of other children in the same situation. Nevertheless, in some hidden fashion he feels that his sister is competing with him too successfully and perhaps he believes that you prefer her. Has he ever said anything about this?

Mother. No, he has never been jealous.

Dr. Adler. In spite of the fact that he wants to be her protector, I believe he is afraid she is developing more rapidly than he is. You see, she tries to protect him also. It is my opinion that Saul will develop better if he is not dominated too much. I should like you to encourage him to believe that he is an important member of the family. Give him ample opportunities for having his own experiences away from home, and consult him occasionally so that you can develop his critical faculties.

MOTHER. I will try to do that.

DR. ADLER. Another thing which is very painful to him is his excessive fat. Perhaps he should have a different diet. Is he particularly fond of sweets?

MOTHER. No, he does not care much for sweets. He drinks milk in school in the morning and then has lunch at noon and dinner in the evening.

DR. ADLER. Does he eat too much bread, butter, and pastry?

Mother emphatically denies that the boy eats too many sweets.

DR. ADLER. If the child is really fat he is assimilating too much, and I suggest that you give him less to eat. The boy's teacher understands him very well and I am sure she will help him. She will be glad to have you consult her if you are in a quandary as to how to treat him.

Saul enters the room smiling and full of confidence, yet a little puzzled by the students. He is dressed in a long trouser suit affected by the younger boys, which makes him look older than he really is.

DR. ADLER (shaking hands with the boy). Hello, sonny, how are you? Won't you sit down here and talk to me? I have some interesting things to tell you.

SAUL. Sure.

DR. ADLER. How old are you?

SAUL. Nine—well, I'm going to be nine.

DR. ADLER. That's fine. I think from now on, you will be able to make very good progress in school. I believe you used to think that you could not be a good pupil.

SAUL. I guess so.

DR. ADLER. But I know that you really can be a good pupil and soon all the old troubles will be gone. You will be more attentive and will understand the teacher better. Then you will get ahead and be well liked in school.

SAUL (impressed). Yes.

DR. ADLER. Do you like athletics?

SAUL. Yes, I do.

DR. ADLER. Is your sister a very sweet girl?

Saul nods in assent.

DR. ADLER. Girls usually develop more quickly than boys when they are young, but you must not believe she is any brighter than you are. You may have believed that she was getting ahead of you, but in a short while you will be able to keep in advance of her. You will always be the older one and will always protect her.

SAUL. Yes, sir.

DR. ADLER. They have told me that you were worried because the boys in the street called you "Fat." When I was your age the boys also used to call me "Fat," but it did not bother me, because I studied hard in school and I told the boys that even when they called me nicknames I got good school reports. What do you want to be when you grow up?

SAUL. I want to be an actor.

DR. ADLER. Then you must learn to read and write, and speak carefully. Even the movie actors must know how to speak well now. I think it would be better for you to study hard than to disturb your class by playing the clown. Wait until you are grown up and are a movie actor, before you try to make other people laugh. Your job now is to pay attention to the teacher and make friends for yourself. Is your mother very strict with you?

SAUL. Yes.

DR. ADLER. You will find that she will not be as strict as she used to be, especially if you get good school reports. Would you like that?

SAUL. Yes.

DR. ADLER (as the boy is leaving). You are a very fine boy.

SAUL (turning at the door and bowing several times). Thank you.

Discussion by the class:

STUDENT. Why did the mother say that the boy never had enuresis, when the boy's earliest remembrance is of being punished for bed-wetting at his grandmother's?

DR. ADLER. The mother explained that this occurrence was unusual. She believed it had been stopped.

STUDENT. What is the significance of this boy having picked for his heroes movie stars who are tall and slender?

DR. ADLER. I do not know these actors, but it is very interesting to hear that they are tall and thin. You see how quickly children find their goal. He wants to be tall and slender because he dislikes being fat. If a child is weak he wants to be strong, if he is poor he wants to be rich, if he is sick he wants to be a doctor because he believes doctors are always healthy.

## *LAYING THE NEUROTIC FOUNDATIONS*

THE student who is presenting the case this evening tells us that the conduct of the patient is a riddle, but we shall do what we can to solve it, in the simplest manner possible.

> "Rachel is a twelve-year-old girl, whose present problem is truancy. She refuses to go to school, on the ground that she cannot work in the classroom."

The opening words of this case history fairly accurately describe a child with an inferiority complex. However, it is not sufficient for us to assume that there is an inferiority complex; we must find all its ramifications and develop a method that will enable the child to compensate for her inadequacies. If Rachel plays truant we may be certain that there are adults in the environment who are attempting to enforce her attendance. The child is saying "No" to these adults, and in this way attains a subjective feeling of inferiority in her home.

> "Rachel has always been a problem child. Her present problem is an extension of her attitude in the class."

"Always" is a very strong word to use, and it is hard to believe that she was a problem from the first days of her life. It is more likely that something happened against which she rebelled. Perhaps this unhappy event was the birth of a younger brother or sister.

> "Rachel was promoted in February to a junior high school with departmental work, from an elementary school where she had been studied and dealt with according to her needs. Rachel cried in her classrooms, and said she could not do the work because it was too hard for her. The teacher of her official class, as well as some of the other teachers, attempted to smooth things out for her, but Rachel insisted that she must return to the elementary school, from which she had been promoted. This she was not permitted to do, because she was expected to meet her problem in her new surrounding."

Crying seems unnecessary, as it would be quite enough if she could not do her work. It is more likely that she cried in order to disturb the class and call attention to her inability. To a certain degree, her reaction is an original one. So original that we may be sure that a girl who is intelligent enough to be in the junior high school at the age of twelve, would recognize that the point would be contested. I am certain that someone, by winning her confidence, could encourage her to face the problem in the class where she is. The fear of being unable to meet her class requirements is hardly likely to be the real reason for her resistance. She has always been a good pupil, and her teachers seem to be kind.

> "Rachel then said she would attend school, if she were permitted to be in a lower class in the junior high school."

Whenever we hear this word "if," we may expect a set of impossible conditions. The real reason Rachel wants to get out of her class and worry her entire environment, is lack of courage to face the new situation. She is boasting of her inability, and the more she insists that she is incapable of doing the work, the more the teachers and parents insist on the contrary. This is one way of turning an inferiority complex into a superiority complex.

> "She was put in a class similar to the one which she had just left in the elementary school, but she did not keep her promise. Her mother went to the elementary school and asked that she be transferred back, but was definitely refused this transfer. Then her father beat Rachel, but she refused to attend. Finally a hearing was called before the Bureau of Attendance, and Rachel was taken to the children's clinic at one of the hospitals. At this clinic, permission was granted her to stay at home for a time."

Rachel's circle of trouble is increasing and it would not be surprising for her case finally to appear in the newspapers. The child was able to make the clinic fall into her trap. It is not sufficient to allow Rachel to stay at home, for she is still the same child, with the same pattern of life.

> "Rachel came to the elementary school to answer the questions for this case history, and brought along a girl whom she seems to have adopted as a friend. This friend's influence is in the direction of inducing Rachel to attend school. Rachel has decided to attend school next fall. Rachel has also said that if she had been permitted to be in the same class with her friend, she would have attended, but this request was refused. Now she is exceedingly worried because her friend will be promoted in June, and Rachel could never get into the same class with her."

This need of being accompanied by a friend and the postponement of a decision to go to school are all symptoms of the inferiority feeling. It is this type of individual who develops a neurosis called agoraphobia, a neurosis which demands constant companionship and support. By cleverly setting her conditions this child has maintained her goal, and put teachers and doctors and parents in an impossible situation. Rachel is the conqueror.

> "Rachel, whose pose is sometimes that of timidity, has showed anything but a meek disposition in the course of her refusals at school. She has been very rude and disrespectful on several occasions."

This interesting evidence confirms my feeling that she belongs to a domineering type, and is not at all averse to fighting others. Her only fear is to meet a new situation alone.

> "As a little girl, there was no fault to find with her conduct, but a year and a half ago, a teacher criticized her work in school."

You see, we must amend the statement that she has always been a problem. Evidently Rachel is striving for an ideal, fictitious goal of superiority. She would like to play God. In order to fill this rôle she must be faultless and domineering, and when she can no longer play that part, she refuses to play at all.

> "At this period she manifested her present symptoms for the first time. She professed to be unable to do her work and was absent occasionally, in spite of the protests of her family, because she said that she was afraid and unprepared. She was allowed to remain at home, on the score of her general health. Recently Rachel revealed that she had harbored resentment against this teacher for six months, before she showed it."

These six months are highly significant, because they were the time of preparation for her neurotic behavior. A neurosis does not appear overnight. It must be nurtured before it can bloom.

> "In February, 1927, when she was promoted, she was not made a monitor in the new class, as she had been in the previous class. This was with a different teacher. At that time, however, she concealed her feelings, so that the teacher never suspected her resentment, and had no fault to find with her. Difficulties began six months later. At this time she remained out of school for some time. In February, 1928, she returned to school and was placed in a slow class with a teacher who was sympathetic and experienced in working with such children. Rachel remained with her for a year, became interested in her work and apparently conquered her timidity. She was encouraged to take part in the assembly exercises and did so to the extent of giving a vocal solo, which she seemed to enjoy. After Rachel became at ease in her classroom she occasionally manifested an attitude contrary to her previous timidity. On one occasion when her teacher could not find Rachel's sewing for her, she became quite impertinent."

You see how easily this girl is able to change her entire behavior pattern when she is in a favorable situation.

> "The parents are living. The family consists of an older sister, nineteen; a brother, seventeen; Rachel who is twelve; a younger sister who is seven years, and a younger brother who is five years old."

We find that she is five years younger than the older boy, and because of this considerable difference in age her situation is similar to that of an oldest child. Her younger sister is five years younger and her little brother seven years younger. Rachel suffered the typical dethronement of the child used to a central position in her family, on the arrival of a little sister.

> "The father rules the family. At one time the oldest son was the father's favorite. The mother has no favorites, but as the children grew older, she had conflicts with all of them."

Probably the mother got along well enough with the children while they were little and she could give them what they wanted. As they grew older, and that was no longer possible, they became troublesome. Perhaps Rachel has been sick, too, and so has had more than her share of indulgence.

> "The children do not tease each other, but Rachel seems to be the ugly duckling."

"Ugly duckling" probably means that she is irritable and domineering. It is quite likely that she causes dissension among the others.

"The older brother has a habit of biting his nails, and when Rachel sees him do this she becomes quite upset and screams. The brother realizes Rachel's nervous state but does not stop biting his nails. The mother is helpless in the entire situation. The oldest sister is very good to Rachel and assumes a motherly attitude toward her. She made a dress for Rachel and took her to the movies. Rachel seems to appreciate that the oldest sister is good to her. Rachel is friendly with the younger child and plays with her, since this younger sister yields to her, as everyone else in the family does."

More evidence confirming the idea we have formed of Rachel's pattern. She dominates the entire family; when she is crossed, she screams.

"The father and the oldest sister work. There are five rooms in the home, and Rachel sleeps with her oldest sister. The child had a normal birth, was breast-fed for three months, and began having stomach trouble when she was weaned. The child was supposed to have rickets, and during the first three years of her life was taken to the Post Graduate Hospital every week for some months, because she suffered from heart trouble. When she was ten years old she was kept in bed for a short time because of the heart trouble. She has always suffered from stomach trouble, but is in better health now. She does not vomit except when riding on street-cars."

Because of her sickness, every whim was probably gratified, and she learned to make use of her ill health to perpetuate this happy state of affairs. This is demonstrated by her reactions in street-cars. As she cannot command the street-car, she is irritated and she expresses her irritation in terms of her inferior organ system, the gastro-intestinal tract. This may be the beginning of agoraphobia.

"She will not eat at home and prefers to eat at a neighbor's house."

Again the imperfect stomach speaks, this time as an accusation against her mother.

"It may be that the home food is unappetizing, as the investigator found that the luncheon consisted of a bowl of canned salmon, which perhaps would not appeal to a delicate child. The younger sister is following Rachel's example of reluctance to eat at home."

It is also possible that the importance of eating is overemphasized in the home, and the children choose that point for attack against their mother.

"Rachel walked and talked at thirteen months, her tonsils were removed when she was a year and a half old because she had abscesses in her throat. She had measles at a very early age. The mother claims that when Rachel was a baby she was afraid of people and she showed her fear by screaming. According to her mother's report she is clean and neat about herself. She is neat in her appearance in school, punctual in her attendance, and very careful about her written work."

Just as fear was an advantage in her babyhood, so she changes to neatness in school to maintain her favorable situation.

"She is indifferent to the wishes of her family, in that she does not want to go to school. She got along very well with the children in school, to the extent of even being sympathetic with other problem cases, in her second term."

This interest means, "*I* am not a problem case."

"Rachel played with another pupil, Molly, who is in the same class with her, during the second term. Molly is about twelve years old, but not as bright as Rachel and rather a quiet girl; not a leader."

Rachel has evidently been successful in dominating her classmate or their friendship would not continue.

"Rachel does not play games, but attends the movies. Her favorite books and the stories she could relate were fairy stories."

The movies require no social feeling, and enable the child to gain an easy sense of significance by identification with the heroines. The competition in games requires self-reliance and hard work.

> "At the present time she will not go to school, refuses to eat or take her medicine. The mother bought the younger sister a pair of socks and although they were not Rachel's size she took such a strong fancy to them that she deliberately put them on after the father left the house."

The father is evidently a power in the family, but as soon as he leaves the home, Rachel is the ruler.

> "The other children realize her condition, and give in to her. They are considerate and kind to her. Rachel got along perfectly in her last classroom and in elementary school, where she was spoiled to a certain extent. The teacher reported that she exhibited fear when she could not do the work. Once, when she was afraid, she cried and held her hands to her mouth, while they twitched nervously. She was mothered and kept at the teacher's desk, and the rest of the class was warned not to disturb her."

Fear is her strongest weapon. By means of fear she is able to control her environment.

> "She had many difficulties during her first term, but in the second term did not differ from other children and seemed to adjust herself very well."

It is quite apparent that when she gets what she wants, Rachel does not cause any trouble.

> "Rachel's earliest recollection is that when she was three years old, her sister Mary had some roller skates given to her by a friend. Rachel wanted to use them but was not allowed to."

It matters little whether it is socks, or roller skates, Rachel resents the fact that other children have possessions which she does not have.

> "Recently she dreamed that she was in her house and that she had to pass the door of a cellar which appeared dark and menacing to her. She dreamed that she was afraid to go out of the house because she had to pass the cellar door. Her mother was asleep, and the children were warned not to wake her. Some friends were in the house, and the children could not keep them quiet. They awakened the mother, who got out of bed and came toward them armed with a hammer. Rachel took the two younger children, whom she protected, and started to go out, past the dreaded door. A voice came up from the door, 'Go back, she won't hurt you.' She felt reassured and woke at that point."

This dream shows beautifully how Rachel prepares her emotional attitude against leaving the home. This is another symptom of the beginning of an agoraphobia. The dream means that she will pass the door, which signifies danger, only in case of great terror; but the voice comes from the door itself, telling her not to take the menace of her mother too seriously. The dream signifies: "Stay home, even if it is unpleasant. Nothing very serious can happen to you there."

> "Her ambition is to be a typist, and her fear is a fear of colored people."

The fear of colored people would be of little value to her in Vienna, where Negroes are very rare, but in America it is an excellent method of producing anxiety. It is as good as any other reason for not going out on the street.

> "The student's discussion of the case is as follows: Rachel has been a spoiled child and has used her ill health to impose her will on others. She desires to gain power by the exhibition of her weakness. Her dream shows that she has a sense of protection toward the younger children, who are unable to thwart her as her parents do. Her ambition may show desire for self-expression along lines (composition) in which she feels that she can do well. Her school troubles were largely associated with difficulties in arithmetic."

So far as I can see, the student who has brought in this report, has made an excellent digest of Rachel's situation. Discussion with the mother elicited the following additional facts. On the first day that Rachel changed schools, the teacher sent her to the blackboard to write a sentence which she could not write. The child began to cry, and the teacher said, "Stupid, go sit down." When Rachel came home she said: "Mother, I do not want to go to school. The teacher is bad and I don't want to go any more." Since this time she has refused to go to school.

### Conference

The child comes in with the mother.

Dr. Adler. Come in and sit down. How are you? Do you like this place? Does it look like a school?

Rachel. Yes.

Dr. Adler. Everybody likes you here, and they are all looking at you. Does that please you?

Rachel. Yes.

Dr. Adler. I think you are a little too fond of having things your own way, wherever you are. If there is a place where you are not sure of having everyone's attention, you try to make excuses for not going there. You make the excuse that you are afraid of colored people to keep from going on the street. No one can keep the attention of the whole world all the time, but if you are friendly and helpful everybody will like you. I know the teacher told you that you were stupid, but that is not so. I am sure that you are a very intelligent girl. The teachers used to tell me that I was very stupid, but I laughed about it. Anybody can do school work, and we all know that you can do yours. But if you stay at home because of your fear of colored people, I shall begin to think you are not so intelligent after all. If I were you, I should make friends with my father. I am sure he likes you very much. If your parents see that you are interested in them, they will like you much better than if you use all your tricks to show them that you are the most important member of the family. Would you like to be a good pupil?

RACHEL. Yes.

DR. ADLER. I think you could do it in a week if you tried. Will you write me a letter and let me know how you are getting along?

Rachel and her mother go out.

DR. ADLER. I do not know how well the mother or the child understood me, but I believe that you all know what I have tried to do. I should like very much to have someone who is close to Rachel explain her tricks more thoroughly to her and encourage her to give them up. It is obvious that the more the child feels suppressed by the father or the teacher, the more she desires to tyrannize over her family and the school. As soon as she recognizes the futility of her goal, she will improve. I believe that with the cooperation of the teacher, this case has a good prognosis.

(The following is a letter which was received from the child a week later:)

*May 22nd, 1929.*

DR. ALFRED ADLER

MY DEAR DR. ADLER:

This week was entirely a different week. I was outside all the time. I think that my visit to you did me good. Miss X thinks that if you would advise me to do some teaching to small children in Miss X's school would be a good idea. I was called in P. S.—to write this letter. This is the first letter I ever typewrote.

Yours truly,
RACHEL.

## *CONGENITAL FEEBLE-MINDEDNESS*

THIS evening we are to have another one of those difficult cases in which we must determine whether a child is actually feeble-minded or not. You will remember that we have already had a somewhat similar case ("Maternal Domination"), and therefore I shall not go into a detailed diagnosis or a description of the medical symptoms which must be considered. I understand that this boy does not attend school and is not taught at home. He has an older sister who goes to school.

His is the only case of the kind in the family. An intelligence test would be of some value here to determine the level of development. I would not say that the intelligence test which I shall give this evening is the only one, or even the best one, to use; but it will be sufficient to determine whether the child is feeble-minded or not. After the test, I shall examine the child by the method of individual psychology, to learn whether he has a definite style of life—whether his movements, attitudes, feelings, and ideas tend toward a definite goal. A great deal may be learned from a difficult case of this sort.

The case notes state:

> "Sidney is a ten-year-old boy who is unable to read and write and is impatient when anything is being read to him. He has a very poor memory, and there is a question whether he is feeble-minded or not."

The mere inability to read or write is not a sign of feeble-mindedness. The child may have been badly prepared for school lessons. It is true that most feeble-minded children cannot read or write, but if Sidney regards reading as an overpowering task from which he wants to escape, he may be considered an intelligent child. A feeble-minded child would be more likely to stay in school and make no effort to get out of the difficulty.

> "The child has a poor muscular development and bad neuro-muscular coordination, and he is unable to dress and undress himself without assistance."

Here again we must determine whether or not his intelligence is inadequate or whether he wants constant support. If this is a spoiled child, it is a very serious case.

> "He has suffered from rickets and poor dental development. A physician advised extraction of nine teeth a few years ago. He could not walk until he was three and one-half years old, and could not speak until he was five years old."

Rickets is a bone-deficiency disease, and a case which lasted as long as this is usually complicated by other imperfections in the child's constitution. The teeth were probably extracted because of their bad position. It is difficult to decide whether a child who cannot speak until he is five years old is feeble-minded, or merely badly spoiled.

> "He has always wet the bed at night, and still does. He urinates too frequently, especially when in a state of nervousness."

Bed-wetting is common among coddled children, especially if there is a younger brother or sister. He may urinate frequently during the day to gain attention, as if he were saying: "I am not grown up. You must watch me."

> "There is no blood-relationship between the parents. The home atmosphere is good and harmonious. There is no quarreling, scolding or nagging in the house. The boy is very fond of his father. The mother attended business, and a maid took care of the children until about two years ago. The house consists of four rooms, there being two small beds for the children. The religion is Jewish—reform."

Perhaps the fact that the mother was a business woman and did not take care of Sidney made it easier for him to turn toward the father. We must learn from the parents whether the maid was able to win his confidence.

> "There are no early recollections. He dreams sometimes of his grandfather, who died two years ago. It was impossible to find out what manifestations the grandfather had."

He may have been badly shocked by his grandfather's death, which occurred when he was eight years old. Perhaps the child is afraid of death. If it suits a child to be afraid, he dreams of fearful things and trains himself to find the very pictures which cause him to be afraid. This means that someone must always be on hand to protect him. We begin to have some semblance of a pattern of life appearing in this history.

> "He also dreams that he fights and quarrels with his boy friends (he has no girl friends)."

It is usually a coward who dreams of fighting. Children are irritated by their own cowardice, and so, in their dreams and fantasies, they make themselves heroes and prove to their own satisfaction how valuable they really are. After a fashion this is a sort of education, but hardly the best kind.

> "It is his ambition to be a soldier, but he expects to be a policeman because he is afraid that if he goes to war he will be killed. He would like to be a plumber, because he would be working for women."

Here is the fear of death, and more evidence of a positive pattern of life. It is interesting to see how timid children train themselves for warlike pursuits. But Sidney is somewhat fearful lest being a soldier is too much for him, and so he contents himself with being a policeman. His desire to be a plumber indicates lack of courage again. He thinks it is easier to work for women in the descending scale of his ambition—soldier, policeman, plumber. His failing courage is a constant thing. This is not an example of ambivalence. There is no question of whether he will be a coward or a soldier; he is only a coward.

> "It is also his ambition to be a drummer in the army. He can distinguish various kinds of music and associate the musicians with their respective songs. He has only boy friends, usually younger than himself."

When a ten-year-old child wants to have only boy friends, it is usually because he wishes to make the stage on which he plays as small as possible. From his point of view he is quite right, and as he is more friendly toward his father than his mother we may suppose that he is afraid of women, and does not trust them. Perhaps he has suffered at their hands, and we must investigate the mother's attitude toward him. It may be that the mother is more strict with him than his father is.

> "He fears to go to school because the children call him 'Idiot.'"

This is really very suspicious, because children are often surprisingly good judges. On the other hand, they are often cruel and inclined to exaggerate.

> "He asks many questions about everything. He plays ball, marbles, and the like for recreation."

I cannot take it for granted, as the Freudians do, that these many questions have to do with sex. Nor is it likely that he is very anxious for information. It is far more probable that he asks stupid questions in order to keep someone occupied with him.

> "He likes to earn money in order to buy the things he needs, also candy and ice-cream."

This sounds more intelligent.

> "The day's routine consists of the following: Sidney eats his breakfast, and then goes to a near-by garage where he watches the mechanics prepare the busses and watches them drive them. He discusses automobiles with the mechanics. Until recently he could not sleep more than four or six hours at a time. For the last few months he has been taking chiropractic treatments and now sleeps nine hours without waking."

If this has been correctly observed, and the child really does not like to sleep, it may be considered further evidence that he is spoiled. The pampered child does not like to sleep because he hates to lose connection with his grown-up environment.

> "A year ago he dreamed that a picture of his dead uncle was hanging over his bed, and every morning when the child woke up he felt nervous and despondent because he believed the uncle was going to kill him."

Again there are ideas of death, and the fear of death. We can be more or less certain that the child has been badly frightened. Servants sometimes scare children in order to cow them into submission—an extremely dangerous proceeding.

> "He can tell the time but cannot tell the days. He likes funny moving pictures. Mother was told that the child would outgrow his difficulties and that no treatment was necessary."

This case history is rather inadequate, and we must have more facts to complete the record. In the first place, we must know more about his first year and why he became so timid. We want to find out why he was so influenced by his grandfather's death, and why he was afraid that his uncle would kill him. It is also very important to understand the mother's relation to the child. This is one of the cases in which a conference with the parents is essential.

## Conference

The parents come in.

Dr. Adler. We should like to know a little more about your child, especially how he behaves at home.

Father. He likes the street very much, and runs around with his boy friends of the same age. He likes them but he does not understand why they tease him.

Dr. Adler. Do they notice a great difference between him and other children?

Father. Yes. He does not understand things as well as the other children. He is very kind and good-natured and a very lovable child. As far as his behavior in the home is concerned, he is very good and he has a peculiar liking for music. He understands anything with rhythm in it. My wife is more fond of music than I am. There is no musical instrument in the house except the radio.

Dr. Adler. Is he interested in anything else?

Father. He seems to be interested only in music. His ambitions are very peculiar. One day he wants to be a conductor, the next a policeman, and anything that wears a uniform appeals to him.

Dr. Adler. Why does he want to go to work?

Father. So that he can wear a uniform.

Dr. Adler. How does he behave toward the older girl?

Father. They are very much attached to each other.

Dr. Adler. Does he cry out at night sometimes? Do you get up to see him?

Mother. Only when he wants to go to the bathroom.

Dr. Adler. How is he in the morning?

Mother. He gets up alone and starts singing. He is a very happy child at all times. He sings anything he hears over the radio.

Dr. Adler. When he was a younger child, did he look normal to you, or did you sometimes find that he had a vacant look?

Mother. When he was about three years old he didn't seem to grasp things.

Dr. Adler. You didn't notice it before he was three years old?

Mother. Until the end of the first year he acted like a normal child, and then we began to notice that he didn't learn to walk and that he was always listening. Although he could not walk, he was interested in what was going on in the room.

Dr. Adler. How did he behave toward strangers?

Father. He was very friendly with them.

Dr. Adler. Did you try to take him to school?

Father. Not before last year, because we could not teach him the A B C's.

Dr. Adler. Didn't you know that there are schools for retarded children, with especially trained teachers who have a good method of training these children?

Father. We tried to find such a school, but did not succeed.

Dr. Adler. How is the older sister?

Father. She is physically perfect and is graduating from high school this year.

Dr. Adler. Is the boy a timid child?

Father. No, he doesn't seem to be afraid of anything. We have a girl to take care of him who is much more timid than the child, and she is afraid that the other children will strike him. He is not afraid of the dark nor of dogs.

Dr. Adler. I should like to make a medical examination of this child and look at his whole body.

Father. I might mention this: when he was three years old he was playing with another child who hit him on the head with a rake. I do not know whether this caused any damage.

Dr. Adler. Did he faint or lose consciousness, or vomit at that time?

Father. No.

Dr. Adler. Has he any deformities?

Father. I would not say that he is deformed, but he is very thin and his ears protrude.

Dr. Adler. Now I should like to examine the boy.

The parents leave the room.

Dr. Adler. I think we can learn more from seeing the child than from further discussion with the parents.

The boy comes in.

Sidney. Hello, doctor.

Dr. Adler. How are you? What would you like to do when you grow up?

SIDNEY. I would like to be a soldier.

DR. ADLER. Why, we do not want any more wars!

SIDNEY. What do you mean?

DR. ADLER. People are much happier when they have peace.

While this conversation is going on Dr. Adler is examining the boy's head.

DR. ADLER. What games do you play with the boys who are your friends?

SIDNEY. All games.

DR. ADLER. What month do you think it is?

SIDNEY. Today is Saturday.

DR. ADLER. Which month?

SIDNEY. August. (The month is really May.)

DR. ADLER (showing him some coins). Which is worth more, this or this?

Sidney knows that a quarter is worth more than a dime.

DR. ADLER. What is the biggest city in America? Do you know?

SIDNEY. America is the biggest city, England comes next.

DR. ADLER. Would you like to go to school and learn to read and write?

SIDNEY. Yes.

DR. ADLER. I will tell your father where he can send you to school. Where do you live?

SIDNEY. East 170th Street in America.

DR. ADLER. What is the number of your house?

SIDNEY. I forget the number.

DR. ADLER. Could you find your way home alone?

SIDNEY. No.

DR. ADLER. What is this building?

SIDNEY. This is the college.

DR. ADLER. What do they do in such a college?

SIDNEY. They ask questions, and write, and do everything.

The boy goes out.

DR. ADLER. While I have been asking these questions, I have been making a physical examination of this child and I find several stigmata of degeneration. The most important are that he has an abnormally small head which we call micrencephalous, and an asymmetry of the left side of the skull. There can be no question as to the defect in his intelligence. If this boy had a real style of life, he would be afraid, but both the manner of his entering the room and his father's account of his activities show that he is not timid. Feeble-minded children can often be distinguished from maladjusted children by their lack of fear. This child is not intelligent enough to know that he is in danger. You remember one of our other cases, a timid and pampered child who screamed and cried for his mother as soon as he was brought in here? He could hardly be forced to look at me, much less to talk to me. This child's behavior was very different. He entered the room fearlessly and opened the conversation himself. There can hardly be a doubt that he is feeble-minded. I know that your board of education provides a school for such retarded children, and the father should be advised by the teacher who brought in the case to enter his child in one of these classes.

## *THE TYRANNY OF ILLNESS*

THIS evening we shall consider the case of a boy of five and a half years. The record states that his present problem is disobedience, cruelty, overactivity, and that "he cannot catch his breath."

When a child is disobedient, cruel, and overactive, it is quite obvious that these character traits are aimed at someone. It may be safe to assume that Milton's mother is a solicitous and orderly woman who demands a certain amount of cooperation from the child. Milton, on the other hand, is evidently not inclined to yield to her, perhaps because he believes that she has been unjust or harsh to him. His revenge is to choose that very type of conduct which affects her most keenly, for a housewife who wants to keep her house in perfect order would naturally resent the overactivity of a boy who jumps from chairs to tables, pulls down curtains and breaks dishes.

The difficulty in breathing is a protest of much the same sort as cruelty and overactivity. When the boy is overactive he protests with his muscles, and when he cannot catch his breath, he protests with his lungs. We must learn to understand this slang which our various organs speak. However, it is just possible that

Milton has a real case of asthma, due perhaps to some protein sensitization. I should be very much surprised if this proved true, as the respiratory protest would be an important and logical part of this child's pattern.

The case notes state further:

> "Milton is the youngest of three children. There are two older sisters, aged twelve and a half and nine and a half years. The two older girls seem fairly well adjusted, and the youngest child is the chief source of difficulty. The father earns forty-five dollars a week, and the rent of the home is twenty-five dollars a month. The mother does not work. There are four rooms, which are neatly kept, and there are three beds. The family is an orthodox Jewish family."

Perhaps the mother has praised the older children for their orderliness, and Milton has lost hope of ever competing with them. It is very probable that he used to be spoiled. If he had a good deal of sickness, he may have learned that while he was sick he was pleasantly overindulged and has adopted the mechanism of an artificial illness, in order to assure himself of his mother's attention.

> "The older girl sleeps alone, but the boy sleeps either with his father or his mother, more frequently with the mother."

A boy of five and a half years ought to be sleeping alone. If he still prefers to sleep with his mother, it is a good indication that he is too much attached to her. He has succeeded in maintaining his connections with his mother during the night, whereas during the day he engages her attention by means of his overactivity. When a child of this age sleeps with his parents, it is much too easy for him to occupy the center of the family stage. Presumably, the goal of Milton's life is to be watched and favored by his mother. The conflict in this family lies in the fact that the mother apparently wishes her son to be socially adjusted, healthy, and orderly, while the boy is doing his best to remain a baby.

> "Milton's physical development was as follows: he was a full-term baby, and the mother experienced no difficulties at his birth. Does not remember his exact weight at birth. He was irregularly breast-fed, with supplemental feedings from the bottle. He had convulsions at seven months. During his early childhood he suffered from bronchitis, pneumonia, pleurisy, tonsillitis and rickets."

This may be evidence that his parathyroid glands are underdeveloped and that his entire personality is an unstable one. Quite possibly he will recuperate from these defects as he grows older. Childhood convulsions may be very terrifying and Milton has no doubt been very closely watched ever since their occurrence. A child should never be allowed to learn the actual dangers of sickness.

You remember that in the very beginning of the case I advanced the theory that Milton's inability to catch his breath was a protest in the language of the respiratory tract. The information that he has had a variety of diseases of the respiratory tract corroborates this idea. In pleurisy or bronchitis, breathing is extremely difficult, and the sick child presents a picture of agonized discomfort which is very terrifying to a parent.

During his illness, Milton's every breath was the object of attention and solicitude. Now when he finds himself in an unfavorable situation in competing with older and better-adjusted sisters, he threatens his mother with his lungs, so to speak. He says in the slang of the respiratory tract, "Take care of me or I shall be sick and you will be sorry."

> "He was tongue-tied at birth, and the frenum of the tongue was cut. During the early convulsions the mother was told that the child was a Mongolian idiot and that he would never amount to anything."

In my opinion it is seldom necessary to cut the frenum. The family must have realized that the child had a speech defect. The mother was undoubtedly shocked by the idea that he might be a Mongolian idiot. Although we have heard only part of the history, this theory seems unlikely. Mongolian idiots are always good, obedient children. They seldom become problems, because they are very meek and never fight. They occur sometimes in families of very good stock, and there are a number of signs by which they may be recognized. This type of idiot usually has a very small head, a round, uptilted nose and a very broad tongue, which shows many fissures and is frequently so long that the child can touch his chin with it. A dry skin and occasionally webbed fingers or toes are further characteristics.

> "Milton is much attached to his mother, but there is considerable conflict with the older sisters, whom he teases. He is cruel to his sisters and to other children. There is no organized recreation, but he likes to play on the street."

Perhaps Milton was badly spoiled during babyhood or during a period of illness, only to lose the affection and solicitude of his mother as he grew older. Many a mother can practically live the entire life of her child for the first year or two, but later he is forced by the very nature of life to accomplish some independent activity. No six-year-old child can be as pampered as a tiny baby, and the child is quite able to sense the difference in the emotional temperature of his family. As soon as this realization grows, the child will show signs of rebellion.

The older girls probably antagonize Milton, and he teases in retaliation. The case history tells us that the boy is cruel. In psychological language this means that he is discouraged. Very often children with an abnormal tendency to cruelty wreak their power on weak or unsuspecting children and animals, in order to console themselves for their diminished sense of importance.

> "The mother is very much concerned with the child's asthmatic attacks. Milton was referred to the Child Guidance Clinic by a pediatrician who found no organic cause for the asthmatic attacks."

Asthma is very seldom an organic disease in children. In many cases it occurs in children who have had pleurisy or pneumonia, as Milton has had. They dominate their parents by simulating asthma, which is a very terrifying disease to watch, and manufacture strength out of their weakness. Whenever Milton is hard-pressed to show his superiority, or whenever he wishes to attack his mother and gain her attention, he capitalizes on this organic disposition. Asthma is his trump card.

> "The mother complains that Milton is always jumping around, and she is constantly afraid that he will hurt himself. She is oversolicitous in caring for his welfare. He spends the entire morning with his mother, during which he is always in trouble."

This is quite conclusive proof that the boy's behavior is aimed against his mother. He knows that she is inclined to be oversolicitous, and he touches her at her weakest point, by bravado acrobatics.

> "The afternoons are spent in the kindergarten where Milton seems to adjust fairly well. The boy complains that he has no one to play with. Both the father and the mother occasionally beat the child because he refuses to obey them. The boy is constantly surrounded by a wall of, "don't do this" and "don't do that." After he is stopped he usually has an attack of breathlessness. The mother appeals to the child not to have the attacks, because she is sick."

Herein lies the crux of the entire situation. The parents, especially the mother, are so anxious for the child's welfare that they do not allow him to play on the street like other boys. Milton is frustrated in his desire for social contact. If he cannot have boys of his own age to play with, he occupies his mother with his mischief. When she frustrates him in this, he attacks her with his breathlessness. Although this is not a conscious process, the child unconsciously realizes what he gains by these spasms. We must admit that the mother is a good psychologist in that she knows that his attacks are not organic. It would be useless to appeal to the child to cease attacks of organic asthma. One does not beseech a lame man not to limp. However, she follows a bad technique because she places a dangerous tool in the child's hand. She makes her sickness or her health depend upon his whim.

"The boy has a bicycle which was given him by an uncle. He cannot use this bicycle very much because his mother has to carry it down four flights of stairs and she is too weak to do this."

In the beginning of the case it was made clear that the child had rickets—a condition which might have been deduced from his motor hyperactivity. A bicycle would naturally be very important to such a child, and it is probable that he resents not being able to use it.

"Milton sleeps with the covers over his eyes and refuses to sleep alone."

This is a characteristic expression of a cowardly attitude. By covering his eyes he shuts out the hostile world, and by sleeping with the parents he maintains the connection at night that he maintains by breathlessness and hyperactivity during the day.

"Milton's first childhood recollection is, 'I was walking when I was a little baby.' "

The interest in walking is further evidence of the important rôle that rickets has played in his life. This type of child is always very active and must be given adequate opportunities for motor activity.

"Milton's ambition is to be a doctor. He says, 'I want to examine.' He wants to be 'in the big school.' He also wants to learn to write. He has already learned to copy letters, although he does not know their meaning."

A boy who has been as sick as Milton would inevitably value the rôle of a doctor very highly. When a child is sick, the parents must call in a doctor, and after the mysterious examination they follow his instructions implicitly. I must say in many respects my own history is very similar to the history of this boy. I believe that my first desire to be a doctor occurred after I had pneumonia as a very young child. I wanted to conquer death, as I thought the doctor did.

> "Milton does not wash or dress himself, but he can find his way on the streets or run errands. He can recognize his own house."

The fact that he can recognize his own house is an excellent test of normal mentality. The boy does not wash and dress himself, because this keeps his mother working for him.

This is an excellent case that should be very instructive. Our course must be apparent to all who understand the underlying theories of individual psychology. We must influence this mother to make Milton more independent. She must not criticize him so much, and she must hide her fears for his future. We have noted that the boy's behavior is always better away from home, and we must explain to the mother that the boy will improve in a more social environment. She should not be censured, but encouraged to get a new viewpoint.

### Conference

The mother enters.

Dr. Adler. Good evening, madam. We have been studying the story of your boy Milton, and we find that in many things you have been a very careful and conscientious mother. Perhaps your chief difficulty lies in the fact that you are too careful. Don't you think that a boy who is as clever as Milton should wash and dress himself by this time?

Mother. I think he can wash and dress himself, but he takes so long that he would not get to school on time. He makes me very nervous.

Dr. Adler. It would be better if he were late to school a few times and you allowed him to suffer the consequences of his slowness. Have you noticed that he is better when he is away from home, than when he is at home?

Mother. He is much worse at home. He tears down the shades, jumps from the table to the chair, and sometimes overturns the table.

Dr. Adler. It is not hard to explain this. Your boy had rickets when he was a child, and one of the consequences of childhood rickets is great muscular activity. He belongs to a type which must be constantly doing something in order to be happy. Perhaps you can allow him a little more freedom outside of the home. Does he have a bicycle or skates?

Mother. He has a bicycle, but I cannot carry it

down-stairs every time he wants it. I am afraid he will get run over, anyhow, riding it.

DR. ADLER. Perhaps you are a little too cautious. Your boy is intelligent, and if you explain the dangers to him, I doubt whether he would get hurt. This is a fine opportunity to show him how much confidence you have in his ability. I think that if you try this you will see that he rewards you, by becoming more responsible.

MOTHER. What can I do about his jumping around the house?

DR. ADLER. It seems to me that it would be very wise for you to arrange to have the boy join some playground group during the morning. He needs this type of activity. The less you have him in the home with you, the better it will be for his development. Perhaps you can arrange to have some neighboring boy carry down his bicycle for him. I want you to understand that Milton does not have a real asthma, but that he produces these symptoms of breathlessness in order to hold your attention and to threaten you. Did you coddle and indulge him very much while he was sick?

MOTHER. Yes, I had to take very good care of him, because he was so ill.

DR. ADLER. Now he is trying to reproduce the attention and care that you gave him then, by recalling to your mind how sick he has been in the past. We believe that if you disregard and ignore these attacks of breathlessness he will never have any more. In addition, it seems advisable to have Milton sleep by himself. He is too old to sleep with you now. He can grow up to be a perfectly normal boy, if you teach him to be independent now. He must learn from you that you do not prefer the two older girls, and that you expect him to grow up and be a useful citizen.

MOTHER. Is there anything wrong with his mind, doctor?

DR. ADLER. So far as I can see from the history, which your doctor has prepared, there is no trace of Mongolian idiocy in this boy. He is very clever and intelligent, but his trouble lies in his wanting to remain a baby. You must show him that it is better to be a grown-up than to be a baby, and your doctor will help you if you have any difficulties. It is very worth while to try to improve his condition, because if you cooperate with us, I am sure that he will make rapid progress. Now let us see the boy.

The child enters the room, is a little startled by the presence of the students, sees his mother and runs to her side. He will not be separated from her and will not allow Dr. Adler to examine him physically. When Dr. Adler asks him a question, Milton looks up at his mother and says, "You tell." He does not want to look at the doctor and hides his face in his mother's skirts. No amount of persuasion will cause him to speak with Dr. Adler. The mother and the child are sent out.

DR. ADLER. I have always taught my pupils not to listen to what their patients said, but to observe their actions as if they were watching a pantomime. You see, this boy would say neither "Hello" nor "Good-by." He refused to make any contact with me, even though I spoke to him in a very kindly way. This is not necessarily discouraging. The second time it would go more easily. Evidently his physician has understood how to win his friendship, because he was able to get many of the boy's reactions. If any of you have had any doubt as to this child's attachment to his mother, it must be dispelled by the boy's actions. If we had suspended the mother from the chandelier, the boy would have found some way to be close to her. She is his sole support. Not only can he not wash and dress himself without her, he cannot even answer questions.

So far as his so-called asthma is concerned, it is the same attachment to the mother written in a language of the respiratory tract. I have called this phenomenon an organ dialect, when an individual does not express his behavior in words, but in the abnormal functioning of some organ, or organ system. There are many remedies which cure the symptoms of asthma, but they do not cure the patient. If this boy is to be cured, his self-esteem must be increased.

Many of my students have questioned the statement that I have often made, that the pattern of an individual's life is fixed by the time he is five years old.

This case demonstrates beautifully how complete such a pattern may be at the age of five. Milton excludes everyone from his society whom he cannot rule. It is quite possible that he may be petted at school and thus not show the signs of problem behavior during his first years there, but it is almost certain that he will become a problem later on in life, so far as his social, and probably so far as his sexual, contacts are concerned.

STUDENT. Why did the boy cry when you tried to remove him from his mother?

DR. ADLER. You can imagine that an ivy plant that has long been attached to its trellis, fears to be removed from that trellis. Milton's crying is just another expression of his will to power. You must not believe that Milton really loves his mother. He is interested in her only as a parasite is interested in its host. With this difference, when the host does not suit the human parasite, the parasite punishes the host. Many people believe that tears are a sign of weakness, but in this case they are surely a sign of power. Milton does not look, nor listen, nor speak to anyone but his mother, and in his complete attachment to her is the beginning of his neurosis. His whole attitude seems to say, "You can demand nothing of me; I am a sick boy." This child may be a potential suicide or criminal. If he meets very great problems which demand independence and strength, with which he is not equipped, he may later commit suicide. Or, on the other hand, he may project his lack of interest in anyone but his mother against society in the form of criminal contact. I have often noticed that robbers and other criminals have written poems in prison in which they shift the guilt for their crime to their mothers, or blame alcohol, morphin, or disappointment in love, for their shortcomings. They do not have to prove their lack of courage.

STUDENT. How do you approach such a child who will not speak to you or look at you?

DR. ADLER. It is impossible to give you all the little tricks which individual psychology contains in its repertoire of therapeutic devices. In the first place, it is really not necessary to speak to the child in the beginning. If enough is known about the boy to instruct his mother how to act toward him, the child can be influenced without his open cooperation. On the other hand, it would be easy to pique the curiosity of this child by not paying attention to him. He wants to occupy the center of the stage, and if I was to busy myself with a large picture book or some mechanical toy, without noticing him at all, he would soon be unable to resist being interested.

EDITOR'S NOTE: The after-treatment of this case was continued in the editor's clinic. Although it was difficult to gain the mother's intelligent cooperation, she was finally prevailed upon to give the child a greater measure of freedom and independence. She was instructed to leave the room whenever he had an asthmatic attack, as she was completely incapable of being objective about the child's breathlessness. Within two weeks the asthma had disappeared entirely, but Milton had not given up his hope of dominating the environment. He countered his mother's disinterestedness in his asthmatic attacks by developing a compulsive repetitive cough, which his mother promptly misinterpreted again. The child had won his point, for, whereas he formerly had five or six attacks of asthma during a day, he now coughed continually. The child was placed in a hospital, and the nurse was strictly ordered not to pay any attention to his cough. He coughed constantly during the morning of his first day in the hospital. During this time a very good contact was made with the child. He was given a stethoscope and allowed to "examine" some of the other children in the ward who were not too ill to submit to this procedure. This was perhaps the first time that Milton gained a real feeling of significance. The editor asked the child, who accompanied him on some of his rounds, whether he thought a certain boy would get well. Milton imitated the serious mien of one of the attending physicians, and said that the boy was very ill but he felt that he would get well. The child was then impressed with the fact that doctors were too busy curing other people to get sick themselves. On his return to his home the cough reappeared, but as his mother had been encouraged by his condition in the hospital, she paid no attention to it and Milton immediately gave up this particular expression of his respiratory dialect. The following week he appeared with an entirely new set of symptoms: an infinite array of grimaces and facial tics. The interesting thing about this symptom was that the child showed it only when he was in public, in this way causing his mother the greatest embarrassment. The symptoms disappeared again after a few weeks of treatment. Milton was then sent to a summer camp with a letter of instruction to the director. For the first few days at camp he sulked, refused to eat, caused a great deal of disturbance, and was finally sent home because of his complete inability to adjust to camp life. His return to the home was characterized by a greater excess of motor hyperactivity than ever before. A few conferences with the psychiatrist were able to convince the child that he was much better off in camp than at home. He was returned to the camp and for the remainder of the summer made a much better adjustment, chiefly because he was allowed to win a few races and gain a measure of athletic significance. On his return in the fall the boy seemed to have gained a certain amount of self-respect and was placed in school for the full day. Under the supervision of the Child Guidance Clinic and the teacher, Milton has continued to make a good adjustment.